KT-421-964

CONTENTS

CONTENTS

ABOUT THE AUTHOR

Susanne Christian is a qualified and experienced careers adviser who has worked for Connexions in schools, colleges and the community. She has written careers books and contributed to careers websites. Now self-employed, Susanne works as a career coach and employability tutor with all ages, spending much of her time helping people to get their CVs working hard for them. She can be contacted at your. cv.coach@gmail.com.

INTRODUCTION

What stage are you at?

Maybe you're in Year 11 or perhaps Year 12 or 13 (S4, S5 or S6 in Scotland). Either way, you've reached one of those points in your life when you have to make some decisions about where you go from here, in terms of:

- education
- training
- work

or sometimes a mix of two or all three.

The big transition points in school are Year 11 (S4) and Year 13 (S6) as these are the commonest leaving times. That is not to say that students don't leave at other times – you are almost bound to know someone who has left after Year 12 (S5) or even people who left school or college during an academic year.

These are the sort of decisions you are likely to be making during Years 11, 12 and 13 (S4, S5 and S6).

- Shall I stay in education?
- Do I want to stay at school?
- Where's the best place to get the qualifications I need for my chosen career?
- What's the best way to keep my options open?
- Is now the right time to get a job?
- Do I need to do some unpaid/voluntary work?
- Is college the right place for me?
- Should I get a part-time job?

Many of these options involve a move – from school to college, say, or from college to work. Some moves are easier than others. If you're moving into your school sixth form, the staff probably know you and know what you're capable of.

But these transition points often mean moving somewhere different, where the staff don't know you. And some of the choices and courses on offer may be popular – they may have many more applicants than places. This means you can't just walk into the next stage – you may have to *apply*.

This is likely to be true for:

- jobs
- apprenticeships
- further education colleges (including specialist colleges)
- voluntary work
- internships and other work placements
- sixth-form colleges
- sixth forms at other schools.

You may even have to apply for your own school's sixth form – especially if it is popular, offers a good range of courses and gets good results.

So you may be competing with others who want to make the same move towards their education and career goals as you are planning to make.

Many colleges, schools and employers base their application process on CVs. You are reaching the stage where most places you apply to will expect you to have an up-to-date CV, ready to send out.

- It is quite common for an employer, for instance, to ask you bring, send or email a copy of your CV.

Just imagine some scenarios.

Going out costs money and Greg's mum can't afford to give him much of an allowance. Anyway, why should she? So Greg decides to look for a weekend job that will fit in with his studies (and still give him time to go out!). He's in luck – he's only just started looking when he spots a notice in the window of the local convenience store 'Saturday assistant wanted'. Great, that sounds just right. When Greg goes in and speaks to the manager, she says 'Let me have your CV.' But what does she mean? What's a CV?

By the time Greg finds out, someone else will have that job.

Lisa's known for a while that she wants to work in advertising, but she also knows that it's very hard to get into and there's a lot of competition. She knows she might have to do some unpaid work or an internship to get the experience she needs. At a careers event, she meets someone from an agency who sounds interested in offering her a chance to work at his office over the summer. 'Send me your CV,' he says. But Lisa's heard him saying that to other students too. She hasn't got a CV prepared.

By the time she gets her CV ready, all those other people will have sent theirs in.

Sam doesn't want to stay on at school. What he really wants to do is train as a plumber. He knows that an Apprenticeship is the best way to do this to get the practical experience alongside the college training. But he can't seem to find an employer with a vacancy. His dad mentions that he met someone who's looking for a trainee. Sam phones the company straightaway. 'Send me your CV,' says the boss. Sam does better than that: his CV is ready to print out so he takes it to the company office. Next day the boss phones and asks Sam to come in for an interview. The interview goes well and the company takes Sam on as an apprentice.

- Even employers who use an application form may ask for a CV as well.
- If you are approaching employers for a job or placement, they are almost certain to ask for your CV.

Who would you rather be – Lisa, Greg or Sam?

Don't get caught out. Find out what a CV is, how to prepare yours and keep it ready to use. Then you won't miss out.

This book takes you through the process of compiling your CV by telling you what you need to know about:

- what needs to go into a CV (and what doesn't)
- ways of presenting the information
- keeping your CV fresh and up to date
- how to make your CV attractive to employers
- submitting your CV.

It's your choice

There are lots of things about a CV that come down to personal preference. You may want to take advice you are offered or you may not. You are getting to the stage in life where you want to make that decision for yourself.

The important thing with a CV is that it reflects *you*. That's why you need to write your own CV so that it's your own work, you are responsible for it and (most important) you are happy with it. After all, it's you who's going to have to send it to employers, sit with it on a desk in front of you at an interview and, maybe, answer questions about it.

It may be tempting to get someone to write it for you, but it's so much better to write your own.

TIP Taking your time over your CV will help you get it right and will mean you don't make silly mistakes.

Making a start

Reading this book is a good start, whether you read it through from cover to cover or whether you dip in and out. Another very useful thing you can do, if you haven't already, is to start collecting together the documents and evidence you will need to complete your CV and to support it once you start going to interviews. Here are some examples:

- school achievements
- qualifications and credits
- record of key skills/functional skills
- social/sports achievements
- certificates
- personal statements.

Not all achievements happen in school. Maybe you are involved in activities elsewhere. You may have, for example:

- ASDAN or Duke of Edinburgh (DofE) awards
- first aid qualifications
- food safety awards
- music exams
- sports awards, Community Sports Leadership, life saving qualifications
- certificates for voluntary work
- letters of praise or congratulation from events or activities
- a letter from your work experience employer
- reference letters from an employer.

TIP If your school doesn't use a progress file or planner, start your own folder to keep all your documents together in a safe place.

Apart from anything else, this can help you realise how much you've done and how much you have to offer an employer.

Good luck!

1 WHAT'S IT ALL ABOUT?

You've picked up this book and started reading it, so either you've decided it's time to look into writing a CV, or possibly someone's decided that on your behalf. Whichever it is, there comes a point in most people's lives when having a CV becomes necessary.

What's a CV?

For a start, the expression 'CV' is a set of initials so, like any initials, it must stand for something. CV stands for 'curriculum vitae' – that's Latin. It comes from the words for 'course' and 'life', so it roughly translates as 'the course of life'. And that's what a CV is aiming to do – present in written form (either printed or electronic) an outline of your life so far. And as CVs are usually used in a work-related context, we are talking about your work-related life so far.

A quick note: many people know what CV stands for, but it is rarely referred to as a 'curriculum vitae'. You are almost certain to hear it called a CV, so don't worry about how to pronounce 'curriculum vitae'.

A résumé?

You may have heard people use the expression 'résumé'. This is the term used for a CV in the USA. It's a French word meaning 'summary'. So, interestingly, we use a Latin expression and Americans use a French word!

In America, a résumé looks a bit different from a UK CV, but you might sometimes hear 'résumé' used interchangeably with 'CV' over here. Unless you are looking for opportunities in the USA, then a CV is what we're talking about.

But why do I need a CV?

Maybe you need a bit more convincing before you put in all the effort needed to prepare a CV.

We live a world of competition. The job market, in particular, is getting more and more competitive. At the time of writing (2010), according to official statistics there were nearly 2.5 million people looking for work. Sadly, the situation is even harsher for young people: nearly a million of the unemployed total are in the 16–24 age group, which means one in five young people are not in work or training. At the same time, just under half a million advertised job vacancies were recorded (Office for National Statistics, 2010).

Now, seeing the hard facts might come as a bit of a shock to you. But it's best to know what you're up against. It's unlikely that you are going to be able to walk straight into a job – whether you are looking now, when you leave school, or later, after you've completed more study or training.

When an employer advertises a vacancy, you won't be the only person applying. You will be sending in your CV and application with many others – possibly hundreds, for some vacancies.

As you probably know, the world economic recession over the past few years is the main cause of such high unemployment. But there are also some longer-term trends that have been causing changes in the job market over the past 20 or 30 years – since your parents or carers were at your stage in their lives and careers.

Many jobs have disappeared. For example, as industrial processes became automated, fewer people were needed on factory assembly lines. These were often unskilled jobs, which don't require any qualifications. Other jobs are created, for people to operate and maintain the machinery. But these jobs need a higher level of skills and qualifications. So there are fewer jobs and a greater demand for skilled workers.

It's not just factories where this is happening. Thirty years ago most large organisations had a typing pool where letters and other documents were prepared. Nowadays, most office workers have a computer terminal on their desk and are expected to have high-level skills in IT to prepare reports, compile spreadsheets and maintain databases.

So the jobs that are left tend to demand higher qualifications. This means you could face competition for courses, apprenticeships or jobs with training: in fact, for anything you might decide to do after Year 11 (S4), 12 (S5) or 13 (S6).

You need to have the right skills, qualifications and experience and they need to be presented in a way that will effectively get you to the next stage in your career. You need a CV to get anywhere with job applications. But not just any old CV. You need the best CV you can possibly have. What does that mean?

It means your CV must be:

- up to date
- complete
- well laid out
- formatted
- able to show you and your abilities to best effect
- carefully checked and proofread.

There's another 'must': **you must type (word process) your CV**.

No employer these days will expect – or accept – a handwritten CV. This may seem like a strange thing to be saying. As you've grown up with computers, I'm sure you are used to writing most pieces of work on a PC. You'll be used to producing schoolwork and coursework this way. But in case you were thinking that a CV is different, I need to be clear about this. So you need to make sure you can get access to a computer.

Why do employers ask for CVs?

If an employer advertises a vacancy, it means that there is a job to be done. It may be that someone has left the organisation, or is about to leave, or it could be that the organisation has taken on some extra work – a big order or a new project, perhaps. Either way, the organisation is probably left with not enough people to do the work.

The employer wants to fill that vacancy as quickly and effectively as they can. That means getting the right person in to do the job. As we've just seen, there are many people competing for fewer jobs these days, so the employer may be able to choose from many, possibly hundreds, of candidates who want the job and think they can do it.

How does the employer choose? They make their choice based on the information given by applicants. Although some organisations use their own application form to get this information, many still ask for a CV instead of (or sometimes as well as) an application form.

The employer has to make a decision, based on the information you give, about whether you might be a suitable candidate for the job. Over the years, in the world of work, the CV has become the most common written means of putting information about the (work-related) 'course of your life' in front of an employer.

So my CV won't get me a job?

It's unlikely, I'm afraid, that a CV alone will get you a job. Only you can do that, usually by attending an interview. Your CV is there to attract an employer's attention enough to offer you an interview.

How does that sound? Easy? All you need to do is type out what you've done so far at school, preferably without any spelling mistakes, and then send it off!

Well, yes and no. You could do this and it might be fairly easy and not take too long, especially if your keyboard skills are pretty good. But it's like your coursework. You know that if you make an extra effort and work a bit harder the end result will look better, contain more information and be likely to get a higher grade.

Why settle for an F grade CV when yours could be A or even A*?

There are lots of things you can do to make your CV attractive to the employer who is advertising the vacancy. For example, you can:

- use a clear, logical format (Chapter 5)
- present enough detail, but not too much (Chapter 7)
- make sure you have the experience which employers value (Chapter 8)
- make the content of your CV relevant to the particular job you are applying for (Chapter 10).

Before you send off your CV you can:

- use some finishing touches to polish up your CV (Chapter 6)
- create a really professional covering letter to send with the CV (Chapter 11).

And, finally, you can:

- send it to the right organisations (Chapter 9).

Getting help

No one is going to expect you to do this all on your own. After all, you may never have written a CV before. That's where this book comes in. In addition, there is a whole range of people willing to help you through this stage of life. You could seek out the advice of some people; others may offer advice whether you want it or not. Some of these might include the following.

■ **Personal/careers advisers**

These are the professionals when it comes to career guidance. Your personal/careers adviser is likely to have lots of experience in helping people put together a CV. You may not know your personal/careers adviser particularly well – this will probably depend on whether they are attached to your school or college. But they will have a wealth of professional knowledge, access to CV templates, etc. You may find it useful to get a personal/careers adviser to look over your CV at some point.

■ **Careers teachers/careers co-ordinators**

These are specialists too. As well as teaching, careers teachers take a special interest in careers and will have experience of helping students with the choices they make when they move on from your school or college. They will be used to helping people make applications in your local area.

■ **Personal/year tutors**

If you have had the same tutor for several years, they are likely to know you pretty well. Most tutors are only too willing to help with the CV process – in some schools and colleges it is part of their job. Your tutor is likely to be able to help you with, for example, the personal profile section of your CV, helping you to get to the heart of what makes you unique and then helping you to put this into words. Even if you do not need help in compiling your CV, most tutors will be happy to look at the finished product.

■ Teachers

Other teachers may know you well, too. You might approach a particular teacher who you get on well with, or one who has taught you a lot over the years, or one whose opinion you respect. Some teachers will have helped a lot of students with their CVs. Other teachers may only recently have gone through the applications/CV process themselves if they have just done their training or joined the school.

■ Parents/carers and family

They probably know you best of all – sometimes even better than you know yourself! In most cases they will be willing to help you through this stage of your life in any way they can. They want to see you succeed.

■ Friends

They know you pretty well, too, especially if you've known them all through school, college, etc. Friends may be able to offer insights which are useful for your CV by offering a perspective on your character which you hadn't thought of. Or they may help you remember what you've done in and out of school when you're trying to list your achievements.

■ Wider peer group

Your closest friends will know you best and it's natural to ask the opinions of people you like and who like you. But what about other people in your class or year group who don't know you so well or even (dare I say it?) don't like you all that much. It doesn't mean you can't respect their opinion. People you've worked with – perhaps on projects, on Young Enterprise or in a sports team – may have different, but still useful, things to say about you. And what about the person you barely knew when you went on your DofE expedition, who you encouraged to finish the trip, despite their leaking boots and blisters? Don't you think they'll have seen a side of you which your best friend may have missed?

TIP Remember, you want a detached view of how you will come across to an employer, not an ego massage from a lifelong mate. For CV purposes, it's more useful to know how you react in a work-related situation than what you're like on a night out.

■ **Other contacts**

You'll know who these are – although it may take some thinking about. Perhaps there is a family friend whose job involves looking at people's CVs. What a useful person to ask to take a look at your CV. Or there might be someone you worked for, or with, on your work experience or your boss in your part-time job who could give you a perspective on how you are when you're in that work situation.

A word of advice: about advice

Lots of people offer help at all stages of your life, not least when you are trying to make decisions about your future. Whether you've sought the advice or whether it's been offered without you asking, a piece of advice *about* advice is to listen to it first and then decide whether or not you want to take it on board. You may even want to use some of the advice but not all of it.

The same goes for this book. Everything in the book is sincerely written and is designed to help. And there's a lot of material here. But not every piece of advice or hint and tip will be useful to every single reader. So use the bits that seem useful to you.

The ability to decide which information or advice is going to be useful to you is called critical analysis or evaluation. It is a skill you will be developing as you go along. Your teachers will be encouraging you to think in this way.

Something else worth bearing in mind about advice is that you could use different pieces of advice at different times. So read this book and then re-read it from time to time. Dip in and out of it. My guess is that each time you read it you will pick up something different.

CV myths

You'll be told a lot of things about CVs. Some are true and some aren't. Have a look at these statements and see what you think about them.

- Employers read every CV carefully.
- Spelling and punctuation don't matter.
- It doesn't matter what I say, they've decided who to employ already.
- Size doesn't matter: a CV can be any length.
- There is a standard format for a CV.
- Employers don't read CVs: they're more interested in meeting people face to face.
- There is a set order for the information and the sections.
- A good CV will get you a job.
- Everyone makes things up on their CV: it's what you have to do.
- There are certain things you have to say.
- Employers keep CVs on file.
- You attract an employer's attention by doing some-thing different with your CV.

Well, before we go any further, I need to tell you that they're all false! Here is the truth behind these statements.

Employers read every CV carefully

Unfortunately, they don't – they just don't have time. They often get many applications for each job and need to decide quickly who to interview. How quickly? You will see different figures floating around about how long an employer spends looking at a CV – I've seen eight seconds, 10 seconds, 30 seconds, two minutes. It doesn't matter exactly. What matters is that it's not very long. That CV has to make an impact – quickly.

Spelling and punctuation don't matter

As with most written documents (coursework, exam answers, etc.), it pays to get things right. Employers are likely to be much more impressed by someone who's taken the time to check their spelling than someone who hasn't.

It doesn't matter what I say, they've decided who to employ already

False – in most cases. Why would an employer go to the trouble of asking people to send in CVs if they know who they want to employ?

Size doesn't matter: a CV can be any length

There are recommended lengths for CVs, usually one or two sides of A4 – one page is most likely for school or college leavers reading this book. If you have a lot of work experience, do a lot of activities or have a lot of qualifications, you may end up with a two-page CV. Incidentally, even people with long careers don't usually have CVs longer than two sides. That's the usual recommended maximum.

There is a standard format for a CV

There are suggested formats you can use and there are templates throughout this book (and elsewhere), but you will find each CV looks slightly different – and that's OK. As long as your CV is clear and contains all the relevant information, you can choose the format that suits you.

Employers don't read CVs: they're more interested in meeting people face to face

They *are* interested in meeting people face to face – that bit's true. It's the best way for an employer to see if someone is suitable for the job (and it's a good way for the applicant to look at the workplace and the employer, too). But how will an employer decide who they want to meet in the first place?

There is a set order for the information and the sections

The way the information is arranged will depend on your circumstances and your personal preferences. The way the information is arranged and the section headings will vary from person to person.

A good CV will get you a job

Yes, but not on its own. The main purpose of a CV is to get you an interview. Then it's over to you to get the job. The CV paves the way to the interview and attracts the employer's attention enough to ask you to come in for an interview.

Everyone makes things up on their CV: it's what you have to do

There is no need to make things up. It's unwise, unnecessary and, in some circumstances, may even be against the law. So don't do it. The way to write a good CV is to make the best of what you've got and present it in the most effective way.

There are certain things you have to say

The employer just wants to hear the plain facts about you and your skills and experience so that they can see whether you might be suitable for their organisation.

Employers keep CVs on file

Some employers say to unsuccessful candidates that they will 'keep your application on file'. Don't expect that they will. Often this is said kindly to soften the disappointment that employers know you feel when you're turned down for a job. Next time the employer has vacancy, they will expect new CVs from all applicants. After all, you'd rather let them have an up-to-date CV, wouldn't you?

You attract an employer's attention by doing something different with your CV

Your CV needs to show what makes you unique. Apart from that it needs to be simple, easy to read and attractive to the employer. There's no need for tricks such as coloured paper, coloured ink, photos, etc.

What do you know now?

- In today's competitive job market, you will need a good CV.
- Different people in your life can offer different types of help.
- You can listen to advice but you don't have to take it.

2 HOW TO USE A CV

So you've started thinking about preparing a CV. You may have got to this stage because (like Greg in the Introduction) you are looking for a job and suddenly realise that a CV is part of the application process. Greg left it a bit late. If he'd been better prepared, he'd have had his CV ready before he started to look for vacancies.

Maybe you're more like Sam – you want to be ready to take opportunities as they arise. Well done!

In each case – Lisa, Sam and Greg – the employer was asking for a CV because they wanted to know whether each of them was the right person for their organisation. In Greg's case, the job was advertised in a shop window. Sam heard about the vacancy through his Dad and Lisa met someone at a careers event.

As we saw with Greg, Lisa and Sam, the most common use of a CV is in the process of applying for a job. I pointed out in Chapter 1 that your CV isn't likely to get you a job: but it is a key part of the process, aiming to attract the employer's attention enough to offer you a job interview.

Advertised vacancies

By far the most common way to get a job is by responding to an advertised vacancy.

The employer lets people know that they are looking for new staff – maybe one or two new staff members or even many at once, in the case of large annual recruitment schemes.

Vacancies are advertised in many ways and in different places using all types of media, including:

- local newspapers: often free
- national newspapers
- notice boards: especially in shopping centres or shops and supermarkets
- shop windows
- newsagents and corner shops
- agencies
- Jobcentre Plus
- Connexions/careers services.

Of course, there's also the internet. You can find vacancies on:

- company websites
- specialist websites
- general recruitment websites.

It sounds a bit bewildering, doesn't it? It's important to remember that not all recruiters use each of the media to advertise their vacancies. Where to look may depend on what you're looking for, as different types of vacancy are advertised in different ways. Here are some general guidelines.

Source	Good for
Local newspapers	• Local jobs • Part-time jobs • Local apprenticeships
National news-papers, e.g. the *Guardian*	• Graduate jobs • Vacancies across the UK • Specialist jobs, e.g. in the *Guardian* media jobs are advertised on Mondays and Saturdays and technology jobs on Thursdays

(Continued)

Source	Good for
Notice boards, e.g. in supermarkets	• Jobs in that store
Shop windows	• Usually for jobs in that shop
Newsagents and corner shops	• Local part-time work such as babysitting or gardening
Agencies	• Temporary work • Hourly paid work • Often work needing few or no qualifications
Connexions/careers centres	• Local jobs • Jobs with training • Mainly for people aged 16–19
Jobcentre Plus	• Range of local jobs • Usually for people aged over 18

The internet is where most people go first to find anything these days – and looking for jobs is no exception. There are numerous sites advertising jobs in different ways. Again, employers may only use the internet in particular ways. It can help to know where to look before you start, so here are some examples.

Source	Examples	Good for
Organisation/ company websites		• Vacancies across the UK • Details of large annual recruitment drives, such as apprenticeship schemes • Information about the organisation's recruitment process • Internship and work placement opportunities

(Continued)

Source	Examples	Good for
Specialist websites	www.do-it.org.uk	• Voluntary opportunities across the UK
	www.museumjobs. com	• Jobs in museums and cultural heritage
	www.greenjobs. co.uk	• Environmental jobs
	www.yini.org.uk	• Paid industrial place-ments between school and university
General recruitment websites (job boards)	www.notgoing touni.co.uk	• Jobs and training opportunities mainly for those at Level 3
	www.totaljobs. com	• Jobs across the UK in all sectors and at all levels

As I mentioned before, employers don't use all the different methods to advertise a vacancy. When you start looking, though, you may find some repetition. For example, news-papers often have an online version with some of the same ads appearing in the printed paper. If you look at a few general recruitment websites or job boards, you may see what looks like the same jobs appearing several times.

You will find that there is no set format for job ads. A quick look at the jobs page of your local paper will confirm this. In many cases – in newspapers, for example – employers design their own advertisements. On a job board, each job ad has the same format, but the format varies from site to site.

You could see something like this if the employer is only looking for one member of staff.

Assistant Wanted

Saturday assistant wanted
For busy high street coffee shop

Send a CV to:
The Manager
That Café
High Street
Our Town
AY10 2PQ

Closing date: 12 August

If an employer is looking for more than one new member of staff, you might see something like this.

Staff Wanted

For new sports shop opening in September

Full-time and part-time staff wanted

Email your CV to

APerson@anemail.com

By 12 August

Some advertisements give more detail about what the employer is looking for.

> **Busy supermarket has on-going vacancies for Till staff and Shelf stackers**
>
> Must be able to work weekends
> and
> Have customer service experience
>
> Send or bring your CV to
>
> The Manager
> Busystores
> Main Road
> Our Town
> AY3 5XY

In each case the employer is asking applicants for a CV and each advertisement is clear about what applicants should do with their CV.

You may have noticed, however, that there are some differences between the ads, such as:

- some give a very clear closing date
- the employers are asking applicants to submit their CVs in different ways – send it, bring it in or email it (and one gives a choice).

All the information in the advertisement (wherever you find it) is important when you apply for the job. Chapter 10 tells you more about how to use this information to make your application as close as you can to what the employer is looking for (it's called 'tailoring' your CV). Chapter 11 talks about how to use the information in the advertisement as you submit your application to the employer.

TIP Remember to read everything in the advert to get as much information as you can about the job being advertised.

Speculative applications

You can apply to organisations that are not necessarily advertising any vacancies. Just because you have not seen an organisation advertising a vacancy doesn't mean that they are not thinking of taking people on. You may not have seen a vacancy advertised because:

■ you aren't looking in the right place
■ the company is intending to advertise but hasn't done so yet.

So it might be worth sending in your CV anyway. This is known as applying 'speculatively', meaning 'on the off-chance'. Other reasons why you might want to do this:

■ you like the idea of working in that organisation
■ you've heard that they might be recruiting.

Again, as I said with advertised vacancies, the most you can expect your CV to do is to interest the employer enough to ask you to come in for an interview. But it will be your well-written, relevant CV that has achieved this.

You may think this seems unlikely to be successful in getting you a job, but some people do end up with jobs as the result of speculative applications. Anyone who has been successful by this method will tell you that it didn't work first time – they had to put in a series of applications, sometimes a large number, to different organisations.

You are probably most likely to make a speculative application for:

- a work experience placement
- work shadowing
- an internship
- voluntary work.

Applying speculatively has become a well-known and well-accepted way of getting unpaid positions. For people trying to get into particular job markets, working on an unpaid basis is an accepted way of getting the experience they need.

TIP Unpaid work can be essential for getting into some career areas and gives you invaluable insight into a new job before committing to working there permanently.

Chapter 9 has more information about this and how it can enhance your CV.

Paper or electronic?

You may be wondering whether you need a hard copy or a soft copy of your CV. The answer is you will need both. As I've already pointed out, handwritten CVs are no longer acceptable so you will be preparing your CV on a computer.

In the advertisements above we saw that some of the employers asked for a printed CV to be sent or handed in and one employer gave an email address, so you need to have both available.

Automated

There is another way of submitting a CV – by uploading it onto an automated job board. In effect, you are advertising yourself to employers instead of the employer advertising a vacancy. Job boards are usually part of a recruitment website, such as www.totaljobs.com, mentioned before. There are many others, including:

- www.cvlibrary.co.uk
- www.jobsite.co.uk
- www.monster.com.

Application forms

As you may know, using a CV isn't the only way to apply for vacancies. You may already have applied for jobs using an application form – whether on paper, electronic or online – or know someone who has.

Some employers prefer to use application forms rather than CVs. Here are some reasons why this might be the case.

- Employers can ask for the information they want (perhaps different information or more detail than you would put in a CV).
- The employer gets the information in a standard format, which makes it easier for them to compare applications.
- The recruitment process is fairer, as everyone has to fill in the same form.
- Application forms filled in by hand can show the employer how neat the applicants are.

You might be thinking, what use is a CV if I'm going to have to fill in an application form anyway? It's still useful to have a CV prepared. Application forms ask for the same sort of information as you will be putting in your CV so it can be handy to have it all clearly laid out in a single document which you can refer to when filling in applications.

Some application processes use an online, interactive form. In some of these, the pages time out if you don't complete them within a certain time limit. You are likely to find this easier if you have the information in a CV so you don't have to keep leaving the screen to go and search for certificates or work out what date you did your retakes.

TIP Having all your information in a well-laid-out CV can make filling in an application form much easier and quicker.

Other applications

I've said that the most common use of a CV is when applying for jobs, but you may find that you are applying for other opportunities too. While some organisations might ask you to complete an application form, others ask for a CV. They may include:

- apprenticeships
- colleges
- sixth forms.

What do you know now?

- Different vacancies are advertised in different ways.
- You have to check across all types of media to find the full range of vacancies.
- Some employers ask for an application form rather than a CV.

3 WHAT TO PUT IN: AND WHAT TO LEAVE OUT

We've established that your CV will be used by a potential employer to decide whether you could be the person they want to work in their organisation. What information do you need to give the employer?

A CV, remember, is 'the course of your life', so an employer wants to know what you've done in your life so far – keeping it work-related, of course.

They need to know about your:

- education
- qualifications
- experience
- skills
- qualities
- knowledge

and, of course, they need to know who you are and how to contact you.

This is the basic information contained in just about anyone's CV – whether they are just starting out on their career path or whether they have been working for years. But not all CVs look the same.

Let's have a look the CV of Callum, who has finished Year 11. There are two versions with the same information presented slightly differently.

Callum McBride
10 Home Road
Mytown
FR1 2PQ
01323 456789

email: cmcbride1@anymail.co.uk

Personal statement
I am happy to take responsibility
I like learning new things
I can communicate well with people of all ages

Date of birth
10th January 1994

School attended
St Peter's School, Anytown
2005–2010

GCSEs

English	B	Science	C
Maths	C	Art	A
German	C	ICT	B

Other certificates
ECDL
First Aid (Red Cross)
DofE Bronze

Experience
• 2 weeks' work experience at ML Laboratory
• Weekly paper round

Interests
Youth Centre – member of Young People's Voice
School cross country team
Films, reading

References available on request

Callum McBride
10 Home Road
Mytown
FR1 2PQ
01323 456789
email: cmcbride1@anymail.co.uk

Personal statement
I am happy to take responsibility. I like learning new things.
I can communicate well with people of all ages

Date of birth
10th January 1994

Qualifications St Peter's School, Anytown 2005–2010

GCSEs	English	B	Science	C
	Maths	C	Art	A
	German	C	ICT	B

ECDL
First Aid (Red Cross)
DofE Bronze

Experience
- 2 weeks' work experience at ML Laboratory observing sampling, test procedures and documentation
- Weekly paper round

Interests
Youth Centre – member of Young People's Voice
School cross country team
Films, reading

References available on request

The two layouts are slightly different. Neither is right or wrong. Which layout you choose is mainly a matter of personal preference. The important point is that each CV shows the same basic information about Callum:

- what he has done (experience)
- what he can do (skills and abilities)
- whether he is the right person for the job and the organisation (qualities).

As well as layout, CVs also differ in the amount of information they include. Let's see another version of Callum's CV.

Callum McBride
10 Home Road
Mytown
FR1 2PQ
01323 456789
email: cmcbride1@anymail.co.uk

Personal statement

I have been responsible for leading training
sessions for a school team.
I enjoy the challenge of learning new skills in and out of school.
I have developed my communications skills with adults and
other young people through Young Peoples' Voice.

Date of birth
10th January 1994

Qualifications   St Peter's School, Anytown   2005–2010

GCSEs	English	B	Science	C
	Maths	C	Art	A
	German	C	ICT	B

ECDL
First Aid (Red Cross)
DofE Bronze

Experience
2 weeks' work experience at ML Laboratory
- I observed chemical sampling
- I took part in lab testing
- I gained an understanding of documentation

Weekly paper round
- I have been delivering papers and leaflets for 3 years

Interests
- Youth Centre – member of Young People's Voice for 2 years
- Deputy team captain of the school cross country team. Winners of the Area Shield.
- I enjoy reading sports biographies to motivate my training
- I am interested in foreign animated films, particularly from eastern Europe

References available on request

In this CV, Callum has given some more detail in each section, so the employer will get an even better idea of his skills, abilities and qualities. It can be hard to judge how much to write and what exactly to put. Chapter 7 has more about this.

But you've probably also noticed that each version of Callum's CV has the same section headings. The sections that Callum has used are the ones that would usually be found on a CV.

Let's have a look at each section in turn.

Contact details

Most CVs have the person's name and address at the top. This makes sense if you think about it. You want to attract the employer's attention enough that they offer you an interview for the job. If they want to interview you, the first thing they will need to do is contact you. So by putting your contact details at the top of the page, you're making it easy for the employer.

Points to watch

- Give your address in full: the employer may want to send you a letter inviting you to an interview.
- Don't forget your postcode: you don't want that letter to be delayed or go astray.
- Include your landline number (if you have one). If the employer can't reach you on your mobile, they can leave a message with someone at home.
- It's fine to give your mobile number as well: you want to be as sure as you can that the employer knows how to contact you.
- Add your email address too: it may be quicker to arrange the interview by email.

A word about email addresses. It may seem like a big laugh to have a 'cute' email address or one that reflects your hobby, but is an email address like perfectprincess@mymail or bigrappa@mymail going to create a good, businesslike impression when you're applying for a job? There's no right or wrong here, but just take a minute to think about it. It might work best if you keep that sort of email address for your friends and set up a new email account for job applications.

TIP Using your name in the email address helps the employer to keep track of applications – which might help your chances of getting that interview.

Personal profile

Usually the personal profile sits at the top of a CV, just under the contact details. You may sometimes see the personal profile at the end of a CV (especially if the CV stretches over two pages), but it is likely to be more effective here at the top.

Most personal profiles are four to six lines long (perhaps three or four sentences). It is a very important part of your CV. A good personal profile does several things at once:

- catches the reader's attention
- acts as an introduction to your CV
- highlights the important parts of your CV
- summarises the CV
- tells the reader what is unique about you
- tells the reader why you are suitable for the job.

That's a lot of work for such a short section. The personal profile has to be good. If an employer is reading a lot of CVs, s/he may only read the personal profile before deciding which CVs to look at more thoroughly.

It's worth spending time getting that personal profile right. Chapter 10 covers this in more detail.

Education and qualifications

The employer wants to see all the qualifications you have gained. It is important to set out clearly your subjects and the grades. It is also relevant when you took your exams, and you might choose to add where you took them, i.e. which school(s) or college(s).

You may still be waiting for your results while you write your CV. Here is a way of showing this on your CV.

GCSEs 2010	English B	Science C
2011	Maths	Art
	German	ICT
	(awaiting results)	

If you have taken some qualifications and are now working towards some more, you can include this on your CV. For example:

Qualifications

GCSEs	English	B	Science	C	2009
	Maths	C	Art	A	
	German	C	ICT	B	
AS level	Applied Art (Double award)			BB	2010
BTEC	Art and Design	(due for completion in 2011)			

An employer will be interested in any other qualifications you've gained – wherever you took them. So be sure to include all your certificates, awards and qualifications.

You may decide that you want to separate out your academic, school qualifications from the others. Employers are quite used to seeing information presented like this. Many CVs for people further into their careers make a distinction between qualifications gained at school, college or university and those gained through the workplace. In fact, some employers may prefer to see the information separately.

Which method you choose could depend on how many of each type of qualification you have. Look at this.

Education

GCSEs	English	B	Science	C
	Maths	C	Art	A
	German	C	ICT	B

Qualifications
ECDL

As there is only one piece of information under Qualifications, you might agree that it works better to have one section called 'Education and Qualifications':

Education and Qualifications

GCSEs	English	B	Science	C
	Maths	C	Art	A
	German	C	ICT	B

ECDL

TIP Update your CV regularly so that it is always ready when you need it.

Any decision you make now about how to arrange the information can be changed later, when a different arrangement might suit you. In this case, as you gain more qualifications, you could separate them into the two sections.

By the way, if you're confused about whether something is 'education' or 'qualifications', don't worry too much about it. Another way to arrange this information is to list it according to where you were studying. For example:

Qualifications

Anytown High School

GCSEs	2009	English	B	Science	C
		Maths	C	Art	A
		German	C	ICT	B
DofE	2008	Bronze award			
ECDL	2008				

Anytown Sixth Form College

AS level	2010	Applied Art (Double award)	BB
DofE	2010	Silver award	

Yourtown College

BTEC	2011	BTEC Art and Design
	2011	First Aid

Experience

This usually means any work experience you've had – whether paid or unpaid. So this section can include:

- paid work (full-time or part-time, permanent or temporary)
- work experience or work placements
- internships
- voluntary work.

As far as an employer is concerned it's all equally valid in building up that picture of your skills and abilities.

Although it's not a rule, it is a convention that experience is listed in 'reverse chronological order', which means in time order, but in reverse (backwards). The most recent experience comes first. Employers will expect this, as it is how most people organise their CVs. It may confuse whoever's reading your CV if you use a different order.

It is a logical idea – your latest job, activity or other experience is likely to be of the greatest interest to an employer, especially if it is something you are currently involved in.

References

Employers don't just take your word for it. They want to see what's on your CV confirmed elsewhere. Some of this is done by showing them your certificates. But what about the things you are saying about yourself? You may say you 'communicate well' and are 'willing to take responsibility'. The employer will want to check that this is how others see you.

At some point in the application process you are likely to be asked to provide the names and contact details of one or (usually) two people who know you well and are prepared to give you a reference (this is known as being a 'referee'). You will need to decide who is best to use. If you are still at school or college (or have left very recently) it will most likely be a member of staff, perhaps the principal or head, or a tutor or head of year.

If you have started work or work-based training, your employer may be willing to be a referee. Similarly, if you have a part-time job or are doing voluntary work, your supervisor or boss may do this.

If you are involved in activities out of school, this may be another source of referee. For example:

- youth leaders
- faith leaders (church, mosque, etc.)
- sports coaches.

Whoever acts as referee needs to have known you for some time – at least a year or more, if possible – so if you have just started a new course or activity, it's probably better to wait until people know you well before asking them about giving references. There's more about this in Chapter 12.

It makes sense to try to use referees who are likely to give you a good reference by painting a good picture of you to the employer. It's not always possible, though, to choose your own referees. Some employers, for example, like to have a reference from school if you've left recently.

You should avoid using people who only know you as a family friend. Most employers do not accept this sort of personal reference – the person has to know you in some kind of work-related context. So you cannot use your neighbour, even if you've lived next door to them all your life, if this is the only way you know them. However, if your neighbour is your youth leader or you work for them in the holidays then it's fine to ask them to be a referee.

You must ask your referees before you give their names and details to employers. After all, it's a matter of courtesy to ask before you pass on any information about a person to someone else. More important, you want to alert them to the fact that an employer may be getting in touch.

TIP It's worth checking that your referee isn't going to be away when the employer is likely to want the reference.

What you don't need to do is put the referees' contact details on your CV. You've probably noticed that none of the CV examples above lists the names and addresses of the people who will give references.

A statement like this is what's needed at this stage.

References available on request

Many employers don't take up references until after the interviews and they will ask you for the contact details when they need them.

TIP Make sure you know the full name, address, phone number and email address of your referees.

Age/date of birth

Does this information need to be on your CV? Yes and no. You do not have to put your age or date of birth on your CV, but employers will want to know how old you are. Why's that?

Since 2006, it has been illegal for employers to discriminate against anyone on the grounds of age. This means that, generally, employers cannot use the reason that someone is too young (or to old) as an excuse for not selecting them for a job. However, like most things where the law is concerned, it's not quite as simple as that. The law also covers the type of work which young people are allowed to do at certain ages.

- If you are under the school leaving age you can only work a certain number of hours each day and at particular times.
- If you are aged under 18, you cannot serve alcohol.
- Generally, if you are under 18 you are not allowed to work nights.

There are other restrictions that apply at different ages. They are designed to protect young people from harm through dangerous work or working long hours. (Some of the laws vary in different parts of the UK.)

Perhaps you can see now why an employer might be interested in your age. They may, for example, need to be sure that you can do all the tasks the job involves. If you are 15 years old, say, and work too many hours it is the employer who is breaking the law.

So if you haven't put your age or date of birth on your CV you can expect to be asked at some point during the application process (and the employer has every right to ask). Even if you decide to leave this information off your CV, the employer will be able to have a guess at your age by looking at some of the other information – when you started or finished secondary school, when you took your exams, etc.

Interests

The sample CVs for Callum McBride earlier in this chapter had a section listing his interests. This can be a tricky one. Some people include their interests on their CV, others leave them out. Like so much else, it's matter of choice.

The golden rule to apply is:

Will it help me get the job?

Try asking yourself this question. Do my interests tell the employer anything about:

- what I'm like at work?
- how well I can do the job?
- my relevant experience?

The answer might depend on what your interests are and what job you are going for. For example, if you're applying for a job in a record shop, it might be a good idea to include a few details about your taste in music (especially any specialist tastes). For an office job, it's less relevant.

Don't worry if you don't do a lot outside school or college: if you spend time with your family of friends, that's fine. But there's no need to put it on your CV as it doesn't tell the employer anything that will make you more likely to be invited for an interview.

This is a big subject. Chapter 7 has more information about how to make your interests relevant.

Section headings

You may be wondering why you need to label each section in your CV. After all, isn't it obvious to the reader when they see a list of GCSEs that it's your education they're reading about? Well, it might be obvious, and it might not be so obvious. It's better not to take the risk. Your CV needs to stand out from the others and the best way to do that is by being very clear. Remember, you're trying to make things as easy as possible for the employer so that they will want to interview you for that job.

That's a lot about what needs to go on a CV. There are some things that don't need to be included.

What you don't need on a CV

■ **The words 'Curriculum Vitae', or 'CV' at the top**
There is no need for this. It is obviously a CV, so you don't need to spell that out. In fact, it wastes valuable space which you may need for some important information which might help you get that job.

■ **A photo**
In most cases, an employer will not expect you to include a photo on your CV. If the employer wants a photo they will make this clear in the application details.

What do you know now?

- Education, qualifications, experience, skills, qualities and knowledge all need to be there on your CV.
- You can arrange the information in the way that that best suits you.
- You need to ask the right people for a reference.

4 WHO AM I?

We've looked at the sections of your CV and the information that goes into each section. You want your CV to tell an employer about you and what you can do. Before you can tell anyone else, you have to have a clear idea yourself about your abilities, qualities and achievements.

In this chapter we're looking at what makes you 'you'. In other words:

what makes you different from other people?

and therefore:

what makes you unique?

There are different ways of looking at this – different parts of your personality. For CV purposes, the most useful way is to think about yourself in terms of your:

- ■ attributes: what you are like, your characteristics
- ■ skills: what you can do, what you are good at
- ■ achievements: what you have done.

Here are some examples.

	Attribute	Skill	Achievement
Sunita	Creative	Design	Designed posters for a social event
Jamil	Well organised	Organising events	Organised a charity quiz

(Continued)

	Attribute	Skill	Achievement
Brandon	Reliable	Turning up on time	Never been late for weekend job in two years
Katie	Works well with others	Teamwork	Played in every position in the football team
Jo	Outgoing	Presentation skills	Gave end of term speech
Kelly	Technically minded	Good at IT	Designed a website

Some people know quite a lot about themselves; others find it harder to analyse themselves. What you really need to be able to do is stand back and see yourself as other people see you. If you don't find this all that easy to do, working through the next section of the book may help. It takes you through the process in stages.

YOUR ATTRIBUTES

Attribute means a quality or characteristic – what you *are* rather than what you can *do*.

Have a go at writing a list of words, or short phrases, which describe you. Try five for starters (if you can manage more, that's great). At this stage, don't worry too much about whether these attributes are work-related. We'll look at that later. And, remember, we're not looking at what you are good at (your skills), we're looking at what you're like (your attributes).

I am . . .	

How did you get on?

It's also useful to look at how you come across to other people, which may be the same as or different from your view of yourself – or maybe a mixture of both. As we saw in Chapter 1, it can be useful to get the views of different people.

You could do this:

by thinking what they might say if you asked them

or:

by asking them!

My friends say I am . . .	
My teacher says I am . . .	
My boss says I am . . .	

My family says I am . . .	
My . . . swimming coach youth leader neighbour guitar teacher says I am . . .	

SKILLS

These are the things you can do, things you are good at. Try making a list. (Your record of achievement or folder of certificates might help here.)

	Skill
1	
2	
3	
4	
5	
6	

Of course, you're not limited to six skills. If you can think of more, make the list longer.

ACHIEVEMENTS

Achievements are things you have done, usually by using your skills – or by developing new skills. They can be specific, one-off things you did, or ongoing things you do nearly every day. It can help to think back to the things that made you feel proud – maybe someone said 'well done' or 'thank you' or commented on what you did. Have a look at Sunita, Jamil, Brandon, Katie, Jo and Kelly's examples in the table near the beginning of this chapter.

It might help if you link each achievement to one of the skills you've already listed.

If you find it easy to feel proud of yourself, you may prefer to list your achievements first and then think which skill each shows.

	Skill	Achievement
1	Skill 1	
2	Skill 2	
3	Skill 3	
4	Skill 4	
5	Skill 5	
6	Skill 6	

There is no reason why you can't involve other people in analysing your skills and achievements, just as I suggested you can do for your attributes. Sometimes other people are better at pointing out our skills and achievements than we are. This might be because:

- we are too modest about ourselves
- we forget what we've done
- things we do all the time don't seem like skills.

Putting it all together

Now you've got a list of your attributes, skills and achievements, we need to work out how to translate what you've got into something useful to go on your CV.

If you've asked several people what your attributes are, it's likely that at least some of the answers are similar. After all, wherever you find yourself – with friends, with family, at school, at work – you are still you. You may act a bit differently with your friends from the way you are work (who doesn't?) but you are still the same person. And that's what we're looking at: the real you.

Let's look at Brandon's list of *attributes*.

Brandon says he is:	hardworking a good communicator sociable
His form tutor says he is:	polite considerate towards other people
His boss says he is:	reliable responsible good with customers
His sister says he is:	chatty polite
His best mate says he is:	a good laugh a good friend

Are you starting to get a picture of Brandon? He sounds like somebody who people like to be with because he's fun and sociable as well as being polite and considerate.

It's interesting, too, to see that what Brandon says about himself is reflected in what others say. He says he's hardworking and his boss considers he is reliable (not quite the same, but it's along the same lines). He says he is sociable and his best mate says he's a good laugh.

Sometimes other people point out attributes you may not have noticed in yourself. Both Brandon's sister and his form tutor say he's polite. He hasn't listed it himself, but if two people who know him well say this about him, it safe to say that's how he comes across to other people.

It can be useful to see your attributes confirmed by other people. It can also be useful to have some contrast between the answers people give you as this shows different sides of your character. Although Brandon's best friend says he's good fun, his boss still says he's responsible (and sometimes those two things don't go together).

Using it on your CV

You might be thinking that Brandon has highlighted quite a few different attributes and that his CV might look a bit odd with such a long list. Let's look again at Brandon's list of attributes. Can you see any patterns there? Some of the attributes Brandon has listed can be grouped together because they are either similar or they are different ways of describing the same thing:

- hardworking
- reliable
- responsible

- polite (twice)
- considerate

- a good laugh
- sociable
- good with customers
- a good communicator
- chatty.

When it comes to including all this on his CV, Brandon could use a short phrase to sum up some of the attributes, for example:

Attributes	Could be summed up as:
A good laugh Sociable Good with customers A good communicator Chatty	**Gets on well with people of all ages** or **Communicates well with people of all ages**

By using one of those suggested phrases on a CV, you would be:

- catching the employer's attention
- relating the attribute to what the employer is interested in

and, perhaps most important,

- keeping it work-related.

Keep it work-related

Remember that the whole CV process is all about jobs, so any information that goes on your CV must be work-related. Of course, employers are interested in you as a person, but they will be employing you to do a job, so what they need to know must relate to the world of work.

You saw in the example above how Brandon was able to link 'chatty' and 'sociable' with 'good communicator' to tell the employer that he 'communicates well with people of all ages'.

Sometimes the things that you say about yourself, or other people say about you, don't sound very work-related. But there's always a way to relate them to work. Here are some other examples.

	What they say	For your CV
You say:	• You are sociable • You like trying new things	Good communicator Flexible attitude
Your teacher says:	• You make good suggestions in group tasks • I can always rely on you • You spend a lot of time checking your work	Problem-solver Mature and reliable Pays great attention to detail
Your mum says:	• You know your own mind • You never seem nervous before exams • You've settled down well in your new school	Self-confident Calm under pressure Adaptable to new situations
Your youth leader says:	• You always try hard with new activities	Determined

In the same way, some of your *skills and achievements* may not seem very work-related when you first start listing them. This is particularly likely to be the case when they relate to activities outside school, college or work.

Let's look at some examples of this.

	What do I do?	How is it work-related?
Skills	Babysitting my little brother and his cousin	Child care skills Taking responsibility
	Making cards for birthdays, etc. of people in my family	Creativity Time management
	When the family goes out together, I always get us organised	Organisational skills Planning

(Continued)

	What do I do?	How is it work-related?
Achievements	I researched and booked the family holiday	Research Budgeting Planning Organisational skills
	I organised a surprise party for my mum's 50th	Planning Budgeting Organisational skills Delegating jobs to others
	I laid the patio in our garden	Construction skills Seeing a job finished Planning Budgeting and ordering materials
	I run training sessions for the junior team	Taking responsibility Planning Team work

Negatives to positives

If you worked through the exercises at the beginning of this chapter, you've thought about yourself and what you're like and you've asked other people about yourself. You probably have a list of attributes (and maybe skills and achievements too); and some of these might be similar, like those on Brandon's list.

Some things on your list you might like – and be proud of. But you might find that some of the things that you say about yourself, or other people say about you, don't sound all that positive. They may be honest and accurate, but may not necessarily be what you want to say about yourself to an employer.

As we've said before, your CV needs to reflect you in the best possible light. Applying for jobs isn't just about what you say to an employer, it's about how you see yourself – and how others see you. If you can think good things about yourself and be confident about how you are and what you're like, you will be able to present a confident face to the world.

Let's have a look at how to think differently about yourself. Maybe some of the comments are like this:

- She's . . . **a day dreamer**.
- He . . . **doesn't finish things**.
- She . . . **talks a lot**.
- He's . . . **easily distracted**.
- She's . . . **bossy**.
- He's . . . **impatient if things aren't done right**.
- She . . . **spends a long time on her coursework**.

They're not exactly bad, but you might want to think of yourself more positively than this. Let's have a go.

They say	You could say
She's a ... **day dreamer**.	I like to consider things carefully. I'm creative.
He ... **doesn't finish things**.	I'm always keen to try out new ideas.
She ... **talks a lot**.	I communicate well.
He's ... **easily distracted**.	I'm open to different suggestions. I take an interest in what's going on around me.
She's ... **bossy**.	I like to be organised. I have leadership skills.
He's ... **impatient if things aren't done right**.	I like to follow laid-down procedures.
She ... **spends a long time on her coursework**.	I pay attention to detail. I'm a perfectionist.

There is always a different way of looking at things – there are two sides to every coin.

TIP If you can see yourself in a positive way, you are more likely to be able to write positive statements about yourself on your CV – and be more confident at interviews.

What do you know now?

- An employer wants to know what makes you unique.
- You can think of yourself in terms of your attributes, skills and achievements.
- Everything on your CV needs to be work-related.

5 GETTING STARTED

By now you have some idea of what needs to be on your CV – and what doesn't. You've looked at how you might present who you are and what you've done.

You're at the stage where you're ready to start writing your CV. So where to begin?

Before you start

Like many things in life, it's best to be prepared, so take a little time to make sure you've got everything you need.

■ **Time**
Writing a CV takes time. Don't try to do it when you know you've got to rush out, or if you're distracted by a coursework deadline. It's fine to spend a bit of time on it and then leave it and come back to it. In fact that's not a bad way to approach it as each time you look at your CV you'll see different features which you like or dislike.

■ **Quiet**
If you can find a place where you can work undisturbed, you may find it easier to concentrate. You'll know what conditions are best for you – whether you like to work with music, for example.

■ **Use of a computer**
Even if you prefer to start by writing down your thoughts on paper, you'll need to use a computer at some point. So it's best if you can choose a time when other members of the family aren't waiting their turn to play games or do

their internet shopping. If you need to use the computer at school, in the library or at some other public access point, see if you can book a time slot which will give you long enough to work on your CV.

■ **All your information**
Collecting together all your certificates and everything you need before you start will save time and help you concentrate.

■ **The right frame of mind**
Try not to see writing your CV as a chore or just another piece of homework which someone else has asked you to do. If you approach it positively, it will help you get a better end product. Think of your CV as the gateway to achieving what you want to do with your life.

How to begin

If you're still feeling a bit fazed about how to get started, it might help to use this plan.

Formats

The basic shape (or format) of CVs can look very similar. It is the detail that tends to be different. When you are faced with that blank screen, it can be hard to know where to start and what information to put where. You may find it easier to have some outline CVs to get you going. You can then use them as templates.

TIP The most important thing for the layout is that it is clear and all the information is there. How you arrange the information is completely up to you.

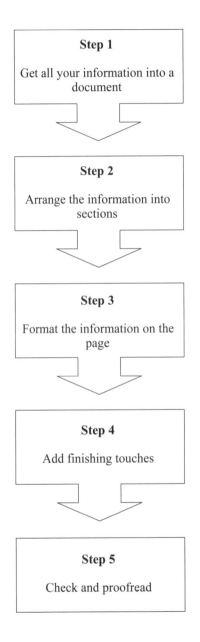

To start with, a very basic format will probably suit you, particularly if you are in Year 10 or 11. Callum is just starting to write his first CV. He has finished Year 11 (S4) so he has his GCSE results. Here are some outlines he could try.

Basic CV format 1

Section headings to one side, no bullets.

Callum McBride
10 Home Road
Mytown
FR1 2PQ
01323 456789
email: cmcbride1@anymail.co.uk

Personal statement   I am happy to take responsibility
I like learning new things
I can communicate well with people of all ages

Date of birth   10th January 1994

School attended   St Peter's School, Anytown
2005–2010

GCSEs

English	A	Science	A
Maths	A	Art	B
German	C	ICT	B

Other certificates   ECDL
First Aid (Red Cross)
DofE Bronze

Experience   2 weeks' work experience at ML Laboratory
Observing sampling, test procedures and
documentation
Weekly paper round

Interests   Youth Centre – member of Young People's Voice
School cross country team
Films, reading

References available on request

Basic CV format 2

Sections headings above, personal statement centred, some sections bulleted, interests centred.

Callum McBride
10 Home Road
Mytown
FR1 2PQ
01323 456789

email: cmcbride1@anymail.co.uk

Personal statement
I am happy to take responsibility. I like learning new things.
I can communicate well with people of all ages

Date of birth
10th January 1994

Qualifications
St Peter's School, Anytown 2005–2010
GCSEs

English	A	Science	A
Maths	A	Art	B
German	C	ICT	B

ECDL
First Aid (Red Cross)
DofE Bronze

Experience
- 2 weeks' work experience at ML Laboratory, observing sampling, test procedures and documentation
- Weekly paper round

Interests
Youth Centre – member of Young People's Voice
School cross country team
Films, reading

References available on request

Basic CV format 3

Section headings above, personal statement and interests justified left.

Callum McBride
10 Home Road
Mytown
FR1 2PQ
01323 456789

email: cmcbride1@anymail.co.uk

Personal statement
I am happy to take responsibility.
I like learning new things.
I can communicate well with people of all ages.

Date of birth
10th January 1994

Qualifications
St Peter's School, Anytown   2005–2010

GCSEs				
	English	A	Science	A
	Maths	C	Art	B
	German	C	ICT	B

ECDL
First Aid (Red Cross)
DofE Bronze

Experience
- 2 weeks' work experience at ML Laboratory, observing sampling, test procedures and documentation
- Weekly paper round

Interests
Youth Centre – member of Young People's Voice
School cross country team
Films, reading

References available on request

Basic CV format 4

Personal statement bulleted, exam results in one column, other sections bulleted.

Callum McBride
10 Home Road
Mytown
FR1 2PQ
01323 456789

email: cmcbride1@anymail.co.uk

Personal statement
- I am happy to take responsibility
- I like learning new things
- I can communicate well with people of all ages

Date of birth
10th January 1994

Qualifications
St Peter's School, Anytown   2005–2010
GCSEs   English   A
                 Maths   A
                 Science   A
                 Art   B
                 ICT   B
                 German   C

- ECDL
- First Aid (Red Cross)
- DofE Bronze

Experience
- 2 weeks' work experience at ML Laboratory – observing sampling, test procedures and documentation
- Weekly paper round

Interests
- Youth Centre – member of Young Peoples' Voice
- School cross country team
- Films
- Reading

References available on request

As you can see, the possibilities for arranging the information are almost endless. The important task at this stage is to get the information about you into a document.

In the end Callum decides to use features from each of these formats.

Callum McBride
10 Home Road
Mytown
FR1 2PQ
01323 456789

email: cmcbride1@anymail.co.uk

Personal statement
I am happy to take responsibility. I like learning new things.
I can communicate well with people of all ages.

Date of birth
10th January 1994

Qualifications
St Peter's School, Anytown   2005–2010

GCSEs				
	English	A	Science	A
	Maths	A	Art	B
	German	C	ICT	B

ECDL
First Aid (Red Cross)
DofE Bronze

Experience
• 2 weeks' work experience at ML Laboratory: observing sampling, test procedures and documentation
• Weekly paper round

Interests
Youth Centre – member of Young People's Voice
School cross country team
Films, reading

References available on request

Once you have decided on your basic format, you can look at some of the finer details of formatting. Chapter 6 discusses this in greater depth.

Which format is best for you?

The formats above are very basic. You can see from the information on them that Callum has just finished Year 11 (S4). A format like one of these will probably suit you if you are just leaving school or if you are still at school.

Callum's sister is in Year 13. She has more detail to include in her CV than Callum. This because she's older and therefore has more experience and because she is becoming more focused on a particular career path. She can start to reflect this in her CV. Here is a format she can use. Again, Kirsty can vary the details of the format by choosing, for example, whether or not to use bullets, where to place the section headings and so on.

Basic CV format 5

Some use of bullets, section headings left justified, profile centred.

Kirsty McBride
10 Home Road
Mytown FR1 2PQ
01323 456789 email: kirstymcb@anymail.co.uk

Profile
Sixth-form student with creative design skills. I am involved in the school centenary art project and have led art workshops at a special needs summer play scheme. I am looking for voluntary work to further the skills and experience I have gained.

Qualifications
St Peter's School, Anytown

GCSEs	English		A
	French		A
	Art		A
	ICT		B
	Maths		C
	Science		C
AS level	English		B
A level	English	(to be completed summer 2011)	
BTEC	Art and Design	(to be completed summer 2011)	

CAD level 2

Skills and Achievements
- Customer service skills in busy supermarket at weekends
- Designed a direct mail leaflet for local company while on work experience
- Organised the design of the sixth-form centenary mural
- Leading art workshops with special needs children

Experience
Supersaver store 2008 – present
Weekend job at Supersaver store including customer service, till duties, shelf stacking and displays. Working overtime where necessary.

Playdays Play Scheme July–August 2010
Assistant Leader of special needs summer play scheme, helping to organise the schedule as well as leading workshops.

Playdays Play Scheme July–August 2009
Assistant at special needs summer play scheme, leading art sessions.

ABC Design May 2007
2 weeks' work experience including production, design and marketing departments.

Interests
Visiting art galleries, particularly new touring exhibitions.

References available on request

Basic CV format 6

Section headings centred, profile centred and justified, minimal bullets.

Kirsty McBride
10 Home Road
Mytown FR1 2PQ
01323 456789 email: kirstymcb@anymail.co.uk

Profile

Sixth-form student with creative design skills. I am involved in the school centenary art project and have led art workshops at a special needs summer play scheme. I am looking for voluntary work to further the skills and experience I have gained.

Qualifications

St Peter's School, Anytown

GCSEs	English	A
	French	A
	Art	A
	ICT	B
	Maths	C
	Science	C
AS level	English	B
A level	English	(to be completed summer 2011)
BTEC	Art and Design	(to be completed summer 2011)

CAD level 2

Experience

- **Supersaver store 2008 – present**
  Weekend job at Supersaver store including customer service, till duties, shelf stacking and displays. Working overtime where necessary.

- **Playdays Play Scheme July–August 2010**
  Assistant Leader of special needs summer play scheme, helping to organise the schedule as well as leading workshops.

- **Playdays Play Scheme July–August 2009**
  Assistant at special needs summer play scheme, leading art sessions.

- **ABC Design May 2007**
  2 weeks' work experience including production, design and marketing departments.

Interests

Visiting art galleries, particularly new touring exhibitions

References available on request

Looking at Kirsty's CV, compared with Callum's, you may have noticed that:

- Kirsty's CV page looks much fuller than Callum's: Callum's page has more 'white space'
- Kirsty has used a smaller font size.

All of this is to be expected – Kirsty is older than Callum, so she has more qualifications (and at a higher level), she's had more experience – paid and unpaid – and she's been involved in more activities, both at school and elsewhere.

And, importantly, Kirsty is starting to use her CV to show what she wants to do. Her CV shows that her interests are in the art and design field, that she has done well in these subjects so far and is taking sixth-form qualifications to build on this. She is also quite clear that at this stage she is looking for voluntary work so she can add to her skills and experience.

I pointed out just now that Kirsty has a lot of detail on her CV. She had to use a smaller font size to fit it on one page. What happens when she wants to add something else? She may well get to the stage where she has too much information for one page.

How long should my CV be?

There is quite a lot of talk about the right length for a CV. It's one of those aspects of CV writing which has almost become a rule. And the 'rule' is that a CV needs to be the right length to show your information clearly and concisely. What this is likely to mean is:

no more than two sides

You may be puzzled by this because most of the CVs so far in this book have been on one page.

But it makes sense. The 'no more than two sides' rule applies to everyone. No one's CV should be more than two sides, however long they have been working, however much experience they have or however interesting their life has been. So most adults try to keep their CVs to two sides.

Someone like you, if you're just starting out on a life of qualifications, skills and experience, is bound to have less to put on a CV. So at this stage your CV is likely to be only one side. I would go further than that and say that employers will only expect one page from someone still at school.

As we've seen with Kirsty, there comes a point when you have to decide whether to squeeze a bit more into that one side or start using a second side. When Kirsty starts to do some voluntary work, she will want to put that on her CV. She can decide whether to create a bit more space on that one page or go on to two.

For the time being she's decided to stick with one side, which she could do by reducing the font size on the profile.

Kirsty McBride
10 Home Road
Mytown FR1 2PQ
01323 456789 email: kirstymcb@anymail.co.uk

Profile
Sixth-form student with creative design skills. I am involved in the school centenary art project and have led art workshops at a special needs summer play scheme. I am now volunteering at an art club to build on my experience.

Qualifications
St Peter's School, Anytown

GCSEs	English	A
	French	A
	Art	A
	ICT	B
	Maths	C
	Science	C
AS level	English	B
A level	English	(to be completed summer 2011)
BTEC	Art and Design	(to be completed summer 2011)

CAD level 2

Experience

Anytown Museum Art Club 2010 – present
Designing and leading weekly after school art sessions for 8–9 year olds, as a volunteer.

Supersaver store 2008 – present
Weekend job at Supersaver store including customer service, till duties, shelf stacking and displays. Working overtime where necessary.

Playdays Play Scheme July–August 2010
Assistant Leader of special needs summer play scheme, helping to organise the schedule as well as leading workshops.

Playdays Play Scheme July–August 2009
Assistant at special needs summer play scheme, leading art sessions.

ABC Design May 2007
2 weeks' work experience including production, design and marketing departments.

Interests

Visiting art galleries, particularly new touring exhibitions

References available on request

She decided, though, that she preferred to keep the font size of the profile the same and delete the line space after each section heading.

Kirsty McBride
10 Home Road
Mytown FR1 2PQ
01323 456789 email: kirstymcb@anymail.co.uk

Profile
Sixth-form student with creative design skills. I am involved in the school centenary art project and have led art workshops at a special needs summer play scheme. I am now volunteering at an art club to build on my experience.

Qualifications
St Peter's School, Anytown

GCSEs	English	A
	French	A
	Art	A
	ICT	B
	Maths	C
	Science	C
AS level	English	B
A level	English	(to be completed summer 2011)
BTEC	Art and Design	(to be completed summer 2011)

CAD level 2

Experience
Anytown Museum Art Club 2010 – present
Designing and leading weekly after school art sessions for 8–9 year olds, as a volunteer.

Supersaver store 2008 – present
Weekend job at Supersaver store including customer service, till duties, shelf stacking and displays. Working overtime where necessary.

Playdays Play Scheme July–August 2010
Assistant Leader of special needs summer play scheme, helping to organise the schedule as well as leading workshops.

Playdays Play Scheme July–August 2009
Assistant at special needs summer play scheme, leading art sessions.

ABC Design May 2007
2 weeks' work experience including production, design and marketing departments.

Interests
Visiting art galleries, particularly new touring exhibitions

References available on request

Skills-based (functional) CVs

So far, Kirsty and Callum have both used a chronological format for their CVs. Chronological means 'time-based'. All their experience is listed in time order and any achievements are highlighted within the description of the job or other activity.

Another approach to the layout of a CV is to add a section on Skills and Achievements. Here is Kirsty's example.

Kirsty McBride
10 Home Road
Mytown FR1 2PQ
01323 456789 email: kirstymcb@anymail.co.uk

Profile
Sixth-form student with creative design skills. I am involved in the school centenary art project and have led art workshops at a special needs summer play scheme. I am now volunteering at an art club to build on my experience.

Qualifications
St Peter's School, Anytown

GCSEs	English	A
	French	A
	Art	A
	ICT	B
	Maths	C
	Science	C
AS level	English	B
A level	English	(to be completed summer 2011)
BTEC	Art and Design	(to be completed summer 2011)

CAD level 2

Skills and Achievements
- Customer service skills in busy supermarket at weekends
- Designed a direct mail leaflet for local company while on work experience
- Organised the design of the sixth form's centenary mural
- Leading art workshops with special needs children

Experience
Anytown Museum Art Club 2010 – present
Designing and leading weekly after school art sessions for 8–9 year olds, as a volunteer.

Supersaver store 2008 – present
Weekend job at Supersaver store including customer service, till duties, shelf stacking and displays. Working overtime where necessary.

Playdays Play Scheme July – August 2010
Assistant Leader of special needs summer play scheme, helping to organise the schedule as well as leading workshops.

Playdays Play Scheme July – August 2009
Assistant at special needs summer play scheme, leading art sessions.

ABC Design May 2007
2 weeks' work experience including production, design and marketing departments.

Interests
Visiting art galleries, particularly new touring exhibitions.

References available on request.

Kirsty has taken her skills and achievements from different parts of her experience and listed them clearly, using bullets. This is likely to catch the reader's attention as they skim over Kirsty's CV.

She could have listed these skills and achievements separately under the relevant job or activity. Each skill or achievement would still be there on her CV, but they would probably have less impact on the employer. It looks very impressive when there are several achievements listed together.

When you progress a bit further and have several skills and a handful of achievements, the list may start to get rather long. For example, Kirsty's list might soon look like this:

Skills and achievements
- Customer service skills in busy supermarket at weekends
- Team-leading skills during holiday cover on weekend shifts
- Leading art workshops with special needs children
- Presentation skills on museum education programme
- Designed a direct mail leaflet for local company while on work experience
- Organised the design of the sixth form's centenary mural

It's still an impressive list. But long lists are less easy to read and less eye-catching. We want to make sure that we attract the employer's attention, so you may want to separate your skills and achievements into two sections. (Remember, skills are things you are good at and achievements are things you have done.)

Kirsty's lists might look like this:

Skills
- Customer service skills in busy supermarket at weekends
- Team-leading skills during holiday cover on weekend shifts
- Presentation skills on museum education programme

> **Achievements**
> • Designed a direct mail leaflet for local company while on work experience
> • Organised the design of the sixth form's centenary mural
> • Leading art workshops with special needs children

With the information arranged as you wish, you can now look at some of the finer details to make it stand out when the employer reads it.

What do you know now?

- ■ It takes time to write a CV.
- ■ You can choose the format of your CV.
- ■ Different formats might suit you at different times.

6 FINISHING TOUCHES

So now you've got your information typed out in a Word document. Let's have a closer look at it.

Remember, you want your CV to work as hard as it can for you in attracting the attention of the employer and winning you an interview. As we saw in Chapter 2, your CV is going to be facing fierce competition. You need to do whatever you can to make it stand out and attract the readers' attention.

Some of the points in this chapter may seem very small and fussy, but they all add up to make your CV the best it can be. Why settle for second best when a bit of thought and a few small changes could make all the difference?

TIP It's a good idea to get used to looking at your CV with a critical eye to see if there is anything you can do to improve it.

As well as making your CV clearer, more attractive and easier to read, an employer will be able to see that you have spent time formatting it to get the best out of it. What messages will that send to the employer? S/he might think:

- this person knows how to use a word processing package
- this person can lay out a document well
- this person pays attention to detail
- this person takes time to present themselves well
- this person thinks about what they do, rather than rushing things.

Which might lead them to think:

I am interested in meeting this person
I might even want to employ them

Word processing software

You may only have a basic word processing package, such as Word Pad or Text edit, on your computer or laptop. This really does not give you enough features to be able to produce a professional-looking CV. If this is all you have on your system, it would be a good idea to format your CV somewhere where you can use Word. This might mean using the system at school or college or possibly at a public access point such as a library, community centre, youth hub or any other place in your area where IT facilities are available. If you need to, what about going to a friend's house to use their system for a while? Or is there someone in the family whose computer you could use?

TIP If you possibly can, you need to produce your CV in Microsoft Word (either for PC or Apple Mac).

Font type

What font is it in? Chances are, if you've just finished typing it on your PC or laptop it will be in the system's default typeface. If you are using one of the most common word processing packages – Microsoft Word, Open Office or Wordmac – this is likely to be Times New Roman.

TIP Above all, choose an easy-to-read font in a good size: this will attract the employer to read your CV.

If your system defaults to Times New Roman, you may want to think about changing it. There's nothing wrong with Times New Roman but, remember, we want to make your CV as good as it can possibly be.

Times New Roman is an old-fashioned font based on a printing typeface which was originally used in *The Times* newspaper before the Second World War. It is not considered the most readable font. You want people to be attracted to read your CV, so think about using:

- Arial
- Calibri
- Verdana.

What's the difference? Look at

curriculum vitae and **curriculum vitae**

Can you spot the difference? It looks much clearer on the right (Arial). Arial is what's known as a 'sans serif' typeface, which means it does not have the little curly bits at the ends of each letter.

Try Arial in one part of your CV – the personal profile, perhaps – and see which is going to look clearer to the reader.

You will see, though, that Arial at the same size takes up less space than Times New Roman (and Verdana, if you decide to use that, takes up more space). You will need to take account of this when perfecting the overall look of your CV. Changing the font may be a good idea in the long run but, in the short term, may mean a bit of reorganising and reformatting to get it looking exactly right.

What isn't generally recommended, though, is using different typefaces in the same document. It can make your CV look a bit messy and can be a distraction for the reader. You want the reader to concentrate on the content of your CV – and offer you that interview – not be distracted by wondering which font style you're going to use next.

Font size

Remember, too, that some people's eyesight may not be all that sharp, or they may have dyslexia – so help them as far as you can.

The standard Word packages which default to Times New Roman also automatically set the size at 12 point. If you decide to change the font style, think about the size too. As we saw in the font styles section above, some typefaces are bigger than others.

- If you decide to stick with Times New Roman, don't go smaller than 12.
- In Arial, 12 is quite large, so use 10 or 11.
- Calibri is best in 10 or 11.
- Verdana is large and clear so, again, you can use 11 or even 10.

Going smaller than these font sizes is *not* recommended. It will make the CV very hard to read and the employer may get irritated and stop reading. However, what you can do with font sizes is mix them in your document, as long as you go about it in a logical, consistent way.

You may want to highlight particular information with larger print. For example:

Susan Brown (Arial 14)
14 This Road (Arial 11)
Mytown
AB14 C12
01234 987654
07798 765432
sbrown@hotmail.com (Arial 10)

looks stylish but at the same time businesslike, rather than:

Susan Brown
14 This Road
Mytown
AB14 C12
01234 987654
07798 765432
sbrown@hotmail.com   (Arial 11)

Using a larger font is also a good way to make section headings stand out. Compare these two layouts of the Experience section:

Experience   2 weeks' work experience at ABC Design
              • I spent time in the production department
              • I contributed to a marketing project

              Weekly paper round
              • I have been delivering papers and leaflets for 3 years
                                              (Verdana 10)

Experience   (Verdana 14)

2 weeks' work experience at ABC Design
• I spent time in the production department
• I contributed to a marketing project

Weekly paper round
• I have been delivering papers and leaflets for 3 years
                                              (Verdana 10)

You can see how a simple change in font size makes the heading stand out and invites a reader to look at the information.

Other attributes: bold, underline, etc

Bold is a neat way to make certain pieces of text stand out from the rest. Let's look at the name and address again. This is an alternative to using different font sizes:

Susan Brown
14 This Road
Mytown
AB14 C12
01234 987654
07798 765432
sbrown@hotmail.com   (Arial 11)

It's up to you which you use, but I think you will agree that either looks more distinctive than:

Susan Brown
14 This Road
Mytown
AB14 C12
01234 987654
07798 765432
sbrown@hotmail.com   (Arial 11)

Some people use <u>underlining</u> on their CV. It is probably best avoided. Word processing systems offer it as a feature, but rather than making text stand out it can make it more cluttered. Looking at the name and address again:

<u>Susan Brown</u>
14 This Road
Mytown
AB14 C12
01234 987654
07798 765432
sbrown@hotmail.com   (Arial 11)

probably looks less clear than the version without the name underlined. Even in this format:

<u>Susan Brown</u>   (Arial 14)
14 This Road
Mytown
AB14 C12
01234 987654
07798 765432
sbrown@hotmail.com   (Arial 11)

it's the larger font size rather than the underlining which makes the name stand out.

You will sometimes see text which uses bold and underline together. This is definitely a bad move. Design and typesetting conventions say use one or the other, never both.

There is an exception to the 'avoid underlining' rule. That's for email addresses or for websites. Nowadays most word processing systems recognise 'www' used in a website name and '@' in an email address. The software assumes you want to insert a hyperlink, which it shows in the text by underlining and using a different colour (usually blue). So our CV name and address could become:

Susan Brown
14 This Road
Mytown
AB14 C12
01234 987654
07798 765432
<u>sbrown@hotmail.com</u>

An employer might find this helpful as it means they could email you direct from a CV submitted online. Even on a paper copy, they might like the fact that you made your email address easy to find on the page. Either way, it's your choice. You don't have to stick with something just because that's what the PC defaults to – it's your CV, you choose.

Consistency

When using any of these features – font style and size or attributes such as bold – you need to be consistent, as we saw with the name and address. Again, it comes down to helping the reader (possibly your future employer) concentrate on the content of your CV rather than being distracted by the format or layout.

TIP It doesn't matter whether you choose to use bold or a larger font size to differentiate certain sections or headings, but whatever you choose, do the same throughout your CV.

Have a look at this.

Other certificates   ECDL.
First Aid (Red Cross).
DofE Bronze.

Experience   2 weeks' work experience at
ABC Design
• I spent time in the production
and design departments
• I contributed to a marketing
project

Weekly paper round
• I have been delivering papers
and leaflets for 3 years

Interests
Youth Centre – member of Young
People's Voice
School cross country team
Films, reading

Did you spot all the inconsistencies? This might help:

Other certificates	ECDL First Aid (Red Cross) DofE Bronze
Experience	2 weeks' work experience at ABC Design • I spent time in the production and design departments • I contributed to a marketing project
	Weekly paper round • I have been delivering papers and leaflets for 3 years
Interests	Youth Centre – member of Young People's Voice School cross country team Films, reading

Can you see what I mean?

- All headings need to be the same font size and either bold or not bold.
- Indented text needs to line up.
- Use full stops at the end of each line or none at all (it doesn't matter which).

White space

This is an important aspect of your CV. You cannot fill the entire page with text. There is bound to be some space on the page. Some of it (margins) the computer will put in automatically around the edges of the page, and some you will put in between lines and sections. Chances are you will have automatically pressed return to introduce extra lines between the different sections. Like the other aspects of formatting and layout, you can choose what to do rather than letting the computer do it all for you.

TIP Leaving white space here and there makes the page more readable.

Have a look at these:

Other certificates	ECDL
	First Aid (Red Cross)
	DofE Bronze
Experience	2 weeks' work experience at ABC Design
	• I spent time in the production and design departments
	• I contributed to a marketing project
	Weekly paper round
	• I have been delivering papers and leaflets for 3 years
Interests	Youth Centre – member of Young People's Voice
	School cross country team
	Films, reading

Other certificates	ECDL First Aid (Red Cross) DofE Bronze
Experience	2 weeks' work experience at ABC Design • I spent time in the production and design departments • I contributed to a marketing project Weekly paper round • I have been delivering papers and leaflets for 3 years
Interests	Youth Centre – member of Young People's Voice School cross country team Films, reading

Each example contains the same information. In fact, each has the same amount of white space. But the second example makes much better use of the line spacing and the width of the page. Which example is easier to read?

But think about it. Any piece of white space is not being used to tell your story. You need to strike a careful balance on your CV. On the one hand you don't want it to look cluttered, with every part of the page filled with text, but at the same time, you don't want to leave out important information in order to create space.

How do you know if you've got the balance right? Have confidence: you will know. You've spent a fair amount of time on your CV already and you've probably got a clear idea of how you want it to look. So you will know when you are happy with it and when it's right for you.

TIP Use the computer's print preview facility to look at the layout of a complete page.

Ask yourself the following.

- Does it look cluttered?
- Is there more white space in one part than another? (At the bottom of a page is a common one.)
- Are the line spaces between sections (and between section headings and the information) consistent?

Let's have a look at some whole-page CVs. You could say that this one does the job. It has Sam's information on one page, neatly laid out.

Sam Greene
10 Home Road
Mytown
FR1 2PQ
01323 456789

sgreene@anymail.co.uk

Personal statement	I am happy to take responsibility I like learning new things I can communicate well with people of all ages
Date of birth	10th January 1994
School attended	St Peter's School, Anytown 2005–2010

GCSEs

English	B	Science	C
Maths	C	Art	A
German	C	ICT	B

Other certificates	ECDL First Aid (Red Cross) DofE Bronze
Experience	2 weeks' work experience at ABC Design • I spent time in the production and design departments • I contributed to a marketing project Weekly paper round • I have been delivering papers and leaflets for 3 years
Interests	Youth Centre – member of Young People's Voice School cross country team Films, reading

References available on request

But doesn't this version look better? It contains the same information on the same size page, but uses a better layout, with some simple formatting, and is therefore much clearer and easier to read.

If you were an employer which one would you choose?

Sam Greene
10 Home Road
Mytown
FR1 2PQ
01323 456789
07777 888888
sgreene@anymail.co.uk

Personal statement	I am happy to take responsibility I like learning new things I can communicate well with people of all ages
Date of birth	10th January 1994
School attended	St Peter's School, Anytown 2005–2010

GCSEs

English	B	Science	C
Maths	C	Art	A
German	C	ICT	B

Other certificates	ECDL First Aid (Red Cross) DofE Bronze
Experience	2 weeks' work experience at ABC Design • I spent time in the production and design departments • I contributed to a marketing project Weekly paper round • I have been delivering papers and leaflets for 3 years
Interests	Youth Centre – member of Young People's Voice School cross country team Films, reading

References available on request

Blocks, lines and frames

You may have seen CVs with more sophisticated formatting. For example:

---

lines to divide the sections

---

a frame around the page

These can look very stylish if your IT skills are up to it. But as I've already said in the sections above:

- don't use more than one of these formatting features on your CV
- be consistent in your use of them. For example, if you are using colour blocks for section titles, you need to use them on all section titles.

By all means use these features, but use them with confidence.

Page breaks

If your CV is only one page long, you won't have to worry about page breaks. As long as you take a bit of time to lay out your page so that you are using the space well, your CV will look fine.

As soon as you start to need two pages for all your information you have to be careful about where the page break falls. The whole CV will look so much better if you think about balancing the information between the two pages, rather than filling page one and using only part of page two.

Be careful, too, that your break doesn't fall in the middle of a section, so that some of your GCSEs are at the bottom of page one and the rest are at the top of page two, for example. It's much better to break between sections.

Remember that you are trying to convince the employer that you take care over your work and that you are competent in IT.

Proofreading

By now your CV is so familiar to you that you you look at it without reading any of it. (Did you spot my error in the last sentence?)

TIP Make sure you proofread your CV before you send it to anybody.

This is true of any document you are preparing for someone else to see. I'm sure you are used to checking over your coursework before you hand it in.

You may have spent some time on writing and formatting your CV. Quite frankly, you're thinking, I'm a bit fed up with this and I can't wait to get it done and print it off. Maybe, but you really do need to take a little more time to read through it carefully to make sure there are no:

 speeling mistakes
 typos like th@is or like this..

- punctuation error's
- Americanizations
- impossible information, such as 'Date of Birth 10/02/2009'.

Or any other mistakes!

I'm sure you'll be using the spelling and grammar checking function on your word processing software. But remember, your computer is only a computer, so do your own check as well.

Even better, once you've checked it carefully, ask someone else to look at. That may be a good way for friends to help each other. It's best to ask someone who's eagle-eyed, but whoever you ask will be reading your CV with a fresh eye and therefore they are more likely to see things you may have missed.

There are another couple of checks you could also make.

■ Print it out

It's also worth printing your CV to make sure it still looks OK on paper: that there are no stray full stops you hadn't noticed when you looked at it on screen, that all the margins line up and the tabs are still where you want them to be, for example.

■ Email it to yourself

Sooner or later you will need to email your CV to an employer. It's an increasingly common way of submitting CVs. In the same way that you want to know that your CV looks OK on paper, you also want to know that it looks good when it's emailed. The simplest way to do this is to email it to yourself as an attachment, which is the most likely way you will be sending it to an employer. Again, make sure that the document is still formatted as you want it to be and that nothing's been changed or distorted.

If you've done all this, you could be ready to go.

What do you know now?

- ■ Spending some time on the finishing touches makes your CV more attractive to an employer.
- ■ You can use the formatting tools which you are confident with.
- ■ Proofreading is an important final check.

7 TELL ME ABOUT YOURSELF

If you've been working through the chapters in this book, by now you've got the basics, with a logical, clear layout, perhaps using one of the formats in this book. At this stage, maybe you've looked at the formatting and applied some of the finishing touches – different fonts, bullets, bold, etc.

If so, you're off to a good start. If you needed to use your CV straightaway, you'd have something to hand to an employer. Maybe you have already been using it to apply for jobs.

TIP Keep using your critical eye and every time you look at your CV, ask yourself: could it be even better?

In particular, you need to be sure that you are telling the employer what you've done and who you are in a way that will interest and attract them.

This chapter is about how to present the things you've done and the experience you've gained so that your CV tells the employer as much as possible about you and what you can do. This isn't about writing as many words as possible – it's all about saying the things that will be most useful in getting a job and presenting them as effectively as possible.

Remember that whichever vacancy you apply for, others will be applying too: and for some vacancies, there will be many other applicants. You want to make sure that your CV is one that the employer wants to read: and that it goes into the 'yes' pile, so you are offered an interview.

Let's start by looking at some extracts from the Experience section of Asha's CV.

> **Experience**
>
> **Saturday job in Coffee Café**
> **September 2010 – present**
>
> Duties include serving customers and clearing tables

There's nothing wrong with this, but it's perhaps not very eye-catching. It doesn't tell the employer very much about what the job involved. We've all been in a café and we know what goes on there, but we don't know what tasks Asha did every Saturday.

This time, she's added some details about her job:

> **Experience**
>
> **Coffee shop assistant**   **Coffee Café**
>   **September 2010 – present**
>
> Saturday assistant in high street café
>
> Duties include:
> Providing a high standard of customer service
> Taking customers' orders
> Preparing counter service drinks
> Clearing tables
> Working early and late shifts to cover extended opening hours

Getting better!

It would be even better with a bit of detail about the café added in. This gives the employer an idea of what size of business

Asha worked in, how busy she was on Saturdays and how hard she had to work.

Experience

Coffee shop assistant **Coffee Café**
September 2010 – present

Saturday assistant in busy high street café with over 200 customers a day

Duties include:
Providing a high standard of customer service
Taking customers' orders
Preparing counter service drinks
Clearing tables
Working early and late shifts to cover extended opening hours

---

By now it's starting to look pretty impressive. Once the information is there, it's time for Asha to look at the formatting and those finishing touches. For example, if she decided to use bullets:

Experience

Coffee shop assistant **Coffee Café**
September 2010 – present

Saturday assistant in busy high street café with over 200 customers a day

Duties include:
• Providing a high standard of customer service
• Taking customers' orders
• Preparing counter service drinks
• Clearing tables
• Working early and late shifts to cover extended opening hours

---

Now it's likely to appeal to an employer much more than the simple statement in the first example above. It's fine to start out with that straightforward statement of your experience, but to appeal to an employer and stand out from other applicants, you need to develop your information in the way Asha did above.

You can do this for:

- jobs
- work experience
- school activities
- out of school activities
- voluntary work.

Let's see some examples. Remember Callum in Chapter 3? He spent his two weeks' work experience at ML Laboratory. In the first version of his CV he said.

> **Experience**   2 weeks' work experience at
> ML Laboratory

In a later version of the CV, he's included a small amount of detail telling the employer that he worked in several different departments.

> **Experience** 2 weeks' work experience at
> ML Laboratory
> Observing sampling, test procedures
> and documentation

Could he have told them more?

> **Experience**
> 2 weeks' work experience at ML Laboratory
> Observing the taking of samples
> Taking part in lab testing
> Full understanding of documentation requirements

Or even:

> **Experience**
> 2 weeks' work experience at ML Laboratory, including
>
> • Observing the taking of chemical samples
> • Taking part in lab testing
> • Full understanding of documentation requirements
> • Part of the health and safety procedures

When you are trying to decide what, and how much, to write it will help to think from the employer's point of view. What are they likely to want to know? Here are some pointers.

Paid work

You need to give an employer a good idea of your duties and responsibilities. They will want an idea of what kind of business you worked/are working in, such as:

- large out-of-town supermarket
- small independent specialist retailer
- local branch of retail pharmacist
- main dealer of agricultural equipment
- village stores and post office.

If you can add any figures – like Asha did – that's even better:

- specialist fish restaurant with 30 covers
- solicitors' practice with six partners
- paper round delivering to 50 addresses
- boarding kennels and cattery for 20 animals
- 25-room hotel.

And then the employer will want to know what you were doing on a day-to-day basis.

Don't forget to mention any additional responsibilities, promotions or special achievements. For example:

- working extra shifts to cover staff holidays
- became team leader after six months
- in charge of breakfast service
- worked unsupervised during manager's breaks
- employee of the month.

Work experience

Everyone knows that work experience varies from person to person. Just talking to your friends and those in your year group will tell you this. Some young people spend their week or two watching other people, while others are given 'real' tasks to do – usually the more routine workplace tasks. It is worth telling an employer about any real work tasks you did, especially if you did them unsupervised.

You don't need to give a lot of detail. Look again at how Callum described his work experience. Even the final example is only a few lines long, but tells the employer about the real tasks he did.

It is also worth telling an employer if you arranged the work experience yourself. Perhaps you approached an employer, used a family contact or wrote to your work experience placement as part of your course.

Here is an example of the difference between:

Work Experience
2 weeks' work experience at High Street Veterinary Surgery

and:

> **Work Experience**
> I arranged 2 weeks' work experience at High Street Veterinary Surgery by making a personal approach to the senior partner
>
> During my placement I:
> • watched the treatment of animals
> • watched minor surgery on animals
> • answered the phone on reception, providing a high standard of customer service
> • assisted with the ordering of supplies
> • attended a meeting with a pharmaceutical company rep

School activities

Not all employers will know about the activities that go on in schools. It may be a while since they were in school themselves! It may feel to you as though everyone knows about the projects which are a feature of your school and play a big part in your life: your friends from other schools may have heard of them and adults in your family may be familiar with them. Employers reading your CV may have come across, for example, ASDAN, DofE or Young Enterprise, but they may not know much about them and may not understand what they involve. So you need to tell them.

You can tell them the time commitment, for example. How long it took to get your ASDAN award, or how many hours a week you put in for your DofE Silver. You can tell them about the business skills you picked up in Young Enterprise.

Employers will be interested in other activities in school, too. Have you been involved in, for example, any of the following:

- sports teams
- paired reading with younger years
- school plays and shows
- fundraising
- your school council
- bands or orchestras
- representing the school at public events.

Tell the employer what part you played. There is a big difference between:

took part in school charity event

and:

organised school charity event.

Again, a bit of detail brings it to life. Here are some examples.

- Organised Children in Need day at school.
- Took part in school band tour to Germany, playing clarinet.
- Head of lighting for school summer production.
- Member of committee for sixth-form Christmas dance.
- As a member of Principal's Council, I show prospective parents around the school.
- Secretary of school History Society, responsible for arranging outside speakers for meetings.

And figures are always a good idea.

- Organised non-uniform day, raising £250 for cancer charities.
- Played with school orchestra at series of three public end-of-term concerts.

Out-of-school activities

Again, employers may not know what some of these activities involve. If you go to your local youth centre or hub, for example, you will need to tell them what sort of activities you are involved in there. Do you take part in a range of activities which show your different interests and talents? Do you have any positions of responsibility?

Callum included his Youth Centre activities in the Interests section of his CV:

Interests	Youth Centre – member of Young People's Voice

After he'd written this he had another look at it and asked himself some questions.

- Will an employer know what this involves?
- Could I say more about this?

Putting himself in the place of the employer and answering honestly, Callum is likely to say 'no' to the first question and 'yes' to the second. As a result, he decides to add some more detail to this section of his CV.

Interests
Regular attendance at my local Youth Centre for over 2 years. I am a member of Young People's Voice, involving sitting on a panel with young people from other centres to discuss the running of Youth Centres in Mytown and allocating Youth Opportunity Fund.

When he's written this, he thinks he could tidy it up and make it easier for the employer to read.

> **Interests**
> 2 years' regular attendance at my local Youth Centre, including:
>
> • Member of Young People's Voice
> • Sitting on panel to discuss running of Youth Centres in Mytown
> • Allocating Youth Opportunities Fund grants of up to £1,000 to local community groups

Employers may have come across some of the uniformed organisations, such as Girl Guides, Scouts and Cadets, which have been around for some time. Others they may or may not be aware of – Police Cadets or Fire Cadets, for example. In any case, you will need to tell the employer what the activity involves and your role and achievements.

Other interests and activities

Of course, not everything that you do in or out of school (or college) is an organised activity. You may have other interests or activities which you do on your own or with friends and family. You will want to make sure these are included on your CV, particularly if they are relevant to the vacancy. Examples might include:

- designing websites or computer games
- making or adapting your own clothes
- building or renovating a car
- playing or composing music
- babysitting or caring for family members.

Voluntary work

Employers will be interested to know about any voluntary work you are doing, especially if it's directly related to the vacancy you are applying for, such as:

- volunteering at your local stables or kennels: for work with animals
- being a Rainbow, Browine, Beaver or Cubs leader: for work with children
- helping at a special needs club: for social care work
- sports coaching: for sport and leisure jobs
- publicity for a club or other organisation: for marketing work.

Responsibilities and achievements

Whatever activity you are involved in, remember that employers are particularly interested in:

- positions of responsibility
- achievements.

These might be ongoing, long-term positions such as team captain, team leader, club chair, committee treasurer. But it is also worth mentioning one-off events, too, such as being team captain when the captain was injured or being team leader while the regular leader was on holiday.

Speaking up for yourself

As you read through this chapter, and try to apply it to the information you are putting on your CV, you may be finding it hard to do. Many of us find it difficult to say good things about ourselves and our achievements. This is quite common, and if you feel like this you are not alone. You could be thinking:

- what you're being asked to do sounds like boasting. But it isn't. Telling an employer what you've done in a previous job or in some of your school activities is not boasting. It's just letting an employer know what you can do. You have to tell them, otherwise how can they know?

■ I was just doing my job – nothing special, just getting on with it. Well, yes, but you still need to tell the employer about what you are doing. Again, how else will they know?

These are some of the reasons why Chapter 4 suggests you ask other people about yourself. Other people may find it easier to be realistic about the things you have done.

TIP Remember, your CV is your chance to shine! Don't be too modest – if there's something you're proud of achieving, make sure you include it on your CV!

In Chapter 1, we looked at some of the people around you who are willing and able to help you at this stage and how they can support you. This might be a time when you ask one of them to get involved as you write your CV. You could try asking, say, your form tutor whether they think you have the right balance so that what you are saying on your CV is not too modest.

The whole truth

It is important not to lie on a CV. You are likely to be found out and then what will the employer think of you? That you are the type of person they want in their organisation? Unlikely. They won't offer the job to someone who has already shown they can't be trusted. If you managed to get through the application process and have already started working, the employer can dismiss you. In some cases, lying to get a job can be a criminal offence.

You cannot pretend, for example, to have qualifications you don't in fact have. Chapter 3 pointed out that if you are studying for a qualification, you can add it to your CV as long as you make it clear you don't hold the certificate yet.

Similarly, you should not claim to have experience which you haven't got. For example:

- I have retail experience (when you haven't)
- I have 2 years' experience (when you have none or perhaps only 6 months')
- I have customer service experience in a restaurant (when you worked in the kitchen and had no contact with customers).

Lies about facts are likely to be found out – at interview when you are asked a question or when the employer takes up your references. Imagine the scene. You are at an interview and the employer says, 'Tell me about your experience in retail' and you have to admit you've never worked in a shop. Or the employer phones your referee to ask what you did in the two years you worked there and your old employer says, 'But she only worked for me for six months.'

Sounds embarrassing, doesn't it? There is no need to get into that situation. You don't need to tell lies or 'embroider' the truth. Just make sure you tell the employer all the details about what you have done.

For example, perhaps you have only got six months' experience. What you need to do is tell the employer about what you've done in that time. It may turn out that you've achieved more in that six months than other candidates have in a year or more. So there's really no need to do any more than tell the truth. Just make sure the truth is good and complete.

CV words

Sometimes it's hard to think of the word you need. You may find when you're writing your CV that you know what you want to say but you can't quite find the right word to express it on paper. Or you may find yourself using the same word over and over again. To stop either of these things happening, here is a list of words that could be useful for your CV.

Experience:

Checking
Communicating
Co-ordinating
Creating
Dealing with
Designing
Developing
Directing
Investigating
Listening

Making decisions
Monitoring
Operating
Planning
Researching
Solving problems
Teaching
Training
Understanding

Attributes:

Accurate
Adaptable
Business-minded
Committed
Competent
Confident
Creative
Determined
Energetic
Enthusiastic

Flexible
Honest
Interested
Keen
Patient
Reliable
Self-motivated
Tactful
Willing

And some phrases:

Able to stay calm
Able to work unsupervised
Accepting responsibility
Act on my own initiative
Attention to detail
Follow instructions

Follow procedures
Give instructions
Meet deadlines
Set myself high standards
Work in a team

What do you know now?

- A CV is not the place to be too modest.
- You need to explain your activities to employers.
- You should never lie on a CV.

8 FILL THAT SPACE

When you're writing your CV, it's important to bear in mind what employers are looking for. Chapter 7 showed you how to make the most of the different types of experience you've got and how to expand the information to give the right amount of detail. This chapter is all about how to take that a step further and make sure that your CV covers the information employers want to see.

What are employers looking for?

There are plenty of surveys and reports on what employers are looking for when they recruit new staff, but most of them say much the same things. As we discovered in Chapter 4, this can be broken down into attributes and skills.

Just as a reminder:

- skills are things you can do
- attributes are your characteristics: what you are like as a person.

The *attributes* which employers are looking for include:

- commitment: works hard for the organisation
- confidence: relates openly to all types of people
- dedication: does what's needed to get the job done
- determination: sticks to something when the going gets tough
- an enquiring mind: willing to ask questions
- enthusiasm: shows keenness
- honesty and integrity: takes responsibility for own actions

- motivation: wants to go the extra mile
- pride in the job: pays attention to detail
- reliability: turns up and ensures the job gets done
- willingness to learn: open to new ideas.

The *skills* which most employers seek include:

- achieving goals: meeting targets set by self or others
- analytical ability: using information from different sources and deciding what is useful and what isn't
- commercial awareness: knowing what businesses need to do to make, and save, money
- communication: speaking and writing well and confidently to all types of people
- flexibility: willingness to try new ideas or work in different ways
- initiative: making decisions and standing by them
- leadership: taking charge of situations
- listening: taking instructions and accepting other points of view
- managing multiple priorities: juggling different demands at the same time
- meeting deadlines: getting things done on time
- planning and organising: thinking ahead for self and others
- problem-solving: thinking about things in different ways and providing creative solutions
- research skills: knowing where to look for information
- teamwork: working alongside and co-operating with other people.

Interestingly, employers look for the same attributes and skills from young people as they do from adults, and this sort of list applies at any age or stage in a person's career. So if you have started to develop these skills, you are setting yourself up for a successful future.

Transferable skills

There's a good reason why most employers are looking for the same skills. It's because these skills are what's known as 'transferable' You may have heard the expression 'transferable skills', but what does it mean? I'm sure you know that 'transfer' means to move from one place to another. And that's exactly what transferable skills mean – skills which can move (transfer) from one place to another.

All the skills in the list above are transferable. They apply equally across different jobs, in different sectors and at different levels. It doesn't matter whether someone is packing sandwiches on a food production line, delivering goods in a van, running their own window-fitting business, managing a government department or saving lives as an accident and emergency doctor. Each one uses those transferable skills.

Let's look at a couple of transferable skills and see how they might be used in those different occupations.

	Oral communication skills	Flexibility
Packing sandwiches	Telling the stores assistant more packaging is required	Being willing to work on different parts of the line
Delivering goods	Checking with customers that the order is complete	Picking up an extra order in the middle of the day
Running a window-fitting business	Discussing a customer's requirements with one of the fitters	Scheduling daily work according to the weather

(Continued)

	Oral communication skills	Flexibility
Managing a government department	Giving a press conference	Changing the way the department does its work according to customer feedback
Accident and emergency doctor	Reassuring patients	Working late to deal with a big road accident

You can see that in each job the skill is used in a different way, but it's still the same skill.

Where do I get transferable skills?

The answer to that is that you've probably already got a lot of them. Chances are you're using them all the time. And, like most things, the more you use them the better you get at it – it's called 'developing your skills'.

TIP Many of the skills which employers want to see are used all day, every day.

Let's have a look at this scenario.

The alarm goes off. 'Oh no,' thinks Rajiv, '6:30 already! But I'm glad I set my alarm (*planning and organising*) so I can get my paper round done and be ready for school on time (*managing multiple priorities*).'

When he gets to the shop, the boss says, 'Holly's phoned in sick. I won't be able to cover her round now because I can't close the shop.'

> Rajiv thinks 'Oh dear, he seems in a bit of a fix (*listening*). I really need to get back home in time to sort out my books for school (*managing multiple priorities*). Never mind, I know where they all are (*organising*), so it won't take long (*problem solving*). And I know the shop can't let its customers down (*commercial awareness*). The boss has been good to me – I'll help him out (*teamwork*).'
>
> So he says, 'Okay, that's fine, Mr Besant (*communication*). I'll take First Street, Third Street and the High Road (*initiative*).' Mr Besant replies, 'Would you mind? Have you got time?'
>
> Rajiv calls, 'I'll just have to pedal a bit faster!' (*flexibility*).

It's still early in the morning. Rajiv's not even got to school yet and already he's shown most of the transferable skills which employers want. He didn't think about using them, he just got on with what he was doing.

By the way, it's not just skills that Rajiv is displaying there. Which of the attributes that employers are looking for did you spot? Rajiv showed his:

- commitment: he was prepared to work extra to help out his boss
- confidence: in the way he talked to Mr Besant
- dedication: in offering to take on the extra deliveries
- motivation: he was willing to help out
- pride in the job: service to the customers was important to him
- reliability: he was on time for work so was there to help out when needed.

And I expect that day he was also using his:

- determination: to get him round the extra deliveries he agreed to make.

As usual, we are talking about work-related skills. The example of Rajiv was obviously work-related because it took place while he was doing his paper round job.

But we've seen in previous chapters that 'work-related' needn't necessarily mean only skills that you have developed in the workplace. In Chapter 7 we looked at all the different types of experience you can add to your CV. The same list applies when you are looking at your transferable skills. We could be talking about skills from any of these aspects of your life.

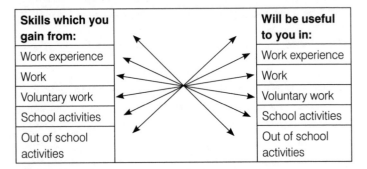

Skills which you gain from:	Will be useful to you in:
Work experience	Work experience
Work	Work
Voluntary work	Voluntary work
School activities	School activities
Out of school activities	Out of school activities

But how does that work? How does a skill I developed at school transfer to the workplace? Like Rajiv, you are using and developing these transferable skills all the time, probably without even noticing. Let's have a look first at which skills you might be using every day at school or college.

Here's another scenario.

Kayleigh walks into school as the first bell is going. 'Phew,' she thinks, 'I've just made it. I'm glad I only stopped to talk to my friend for a minute or two' (*managing multiple priorities*).

In tutor time, after registration, Kayleigh's tutor group start discussing their plans (*communication skills*) for their stall at the school summer fair (*teamwork*).

'I'll be in charge of their publicity,' says Kayleigh (*leadership*), 'unless anyone else wants to do it.' 'No,' the others say. 'You're good at that.' 'Okay' (*listening*). Kayleigh says she will meet with the other tutor groups (*initiative*) to see what they are doing (*analytical ability, research skills*).

She goes to book a session in the IT room. At break she looks at her planner and realises that she has a piece of coursework to hand in next Monday. 'I'd better use the computer time for that instead; I can do the posters later in the week' (*managing multiple priorities*).

Again, just a small snapshot from Kayleigh's day shows her using several transferable skills

Your own transferable skills

You might be thinking, that's fine for Rajiv and Kayleigh, but what about me? These scenarios are intended to illustrate typical events which might occur in the lives of young people. Obviously everyone is different and we all live different lives.

It may help to take each transferable skill in turn and look at some ways in which you may be using and developing it. The questions are intended as prompts to help you think about what you are doing in a way that will be helpful for your CV.

Achieving goals

(Meeting targets set by self or others.)

If you're working towards GCSEs, A levels, AS levels, Highers or any other qualifications; ASDAN, DofE or other achievement awards; or music exams, you are constantly working towards, and achieving, goals. The goal might be getting a particular grade or just getting the work done.

- Are you trying to improve your sports performance, perhaps aiming to get selected for the school's first team or trying to beat your personal best?
- Are you involved in fundraising for a piece of equipment or to pay for a trip overseas?

All these are goals and you are working hard to achieve them.

Analytical ability

(Using information from different sources and deciding what is useful and what isn't.)

You do this all the time. You're doing it as you read this book. Every time a teacher or tutor tells you something and you decide whether or not you agree with them you are using your analytical skills.

If you are working with others, sharing ideas for a project, you will be deciding all the time whether or not you agree with what the other group members are saying. You will also be deciding which ideas are useful for the project and which are not so useful.

- Do you take part in discussions or debates, perhaps as part of your coursework?
- Are you on a committee – in school or out of school – where people put forward their views and the group reaches an agreement?
- Have you been involved in school projects in which you have to produce a piece of work as a group, perhaps in drama or performing arts?
- Have you been involved in Young Enterprise or Young Engineer projects?
- For projects or coursework, do you find information from different sources (internet, books, surveys, etc.) and use only what seems useful for your piece of work?

Commercial awareness

(Knowing what businesses need to do to make, and save, money.)

- Are you setting yourself a personal budget or saving hard, perhaps for driving lessons or a car, or to go travelling when you finish school?
- Are you involved in Young Enterprise?
- Are you taking part in decisions about how to spend money from fundraising?
- Do you have a weekly or monthly allowance or wages and take responsibility for your clothes, books, etc?
- Have you been involved in making any decisions about how money is spent at your youth centre?
- Have you done any work experience in a business environment?

Communication

(Speaking and writing well and confidently to all types of people.)

Communication can be either written or oral. It is possible to have skills in one or other or both.

Oral skills

- Do you do any speaking or performing to an audience (presentation skills)?
- Do you take part in any group activities for your coursework or activities involving working with other people – Young Enterprise or group projects?
- Are you working in a job in which you communicate with customers or colleagues?

Written skills

- Do you write for a school magazine or newsletter?
- Are you taking any GCSE, Standard grade, AS, A levels or Highers such as English or history which involve writing: either essays or in other styles?

Flexibility

(Willingness to try new ideas or work in different ways.)

- In your part-time job, do you have to do different tasks or take on different roles during a day's work?
- Are you sometimes asked to work extra, or different, hours?
- Have you already had several jobs, with different employers? Or are you doing several jobs at the moment?
- Are you called on to help out at home or to care for family members, sometimes at short notice?
- If you do odd jobs such as babysitting, dog walking or gardening, do your customers sometimes want you to work the same day, or even immediately?

Initiative

(Making decisions and standing by them.)

- When working with a group, have you come up with an idea which the whole group has agreed with?
- Have you ever been in a difficult situation and had to decide what to do for yourself and/or others?
- Have you taken part in team-building exercises in which you had to make decisions for the group?
- Did you have to take decisions on your own in your work experience?
- In your part-time job, do you find yourself in situations where you need to make decisions on your own?

Leadership

(Taking charge of situations.)

- Are you captain of a sports team?
- Do you hold a position of responsibility in any of the clubs or societies at your school or college?
- Have you taken any sports leadership qualifications?

- Does any of your voluntary work put you in a position of responsibility for others: either your peers or younger children?
- Were you given responsibility for any tasks during your work experience?
- Are you a member of any of the uniformed organisations: Scouts, Guides, Cadets, etc?
- Have you found yourself in any unexpected, one-off situations where you took charge: a lost child or a first aid incident, perhaps?

Listening

(Taking instructions and accepting other points of view.)

- Have you been on outdoor activities where you have followed the directions of the leader in a challenging situation?
- Are you part of a sports team where you follow the instructions of the coach?
- Have you taken part in group activities where everyone has to listen to each others' views and reach a decision together?
- When you started your job, did you have to learn the procedures from your supervisor or a colleague?
- Do you have to follow health and safety procedures for lessons in the lab or workshop?
- Have you ever had to deal with an 'awkward customer' at work, on your work experience or in your voluntary work?

Managing multiple priorities

(Juggling different demands at the same time.)

- Are you studying several subjects with different teachers? (You may even be studying different courses at different places.)
- Do your courses have different deadlines for coursework?

- Have you taken GCSEs, A levels, etc. and had to deal with a tight exam timetable?
- Are you juggling school (or college) with part-time work, sports training and other commitments?

Meeting deadlines

(Getting things done on time.)

- Do you always get your coursework in on time (or even early!)?
- Are you always on time for school: and anything else you're involved in?
- Do you have a 100% attendance record at school?
- If you have a part-time job, do you have 100% attendance there?
- If you're in a sports team, have you played in every match of the season and attended every training session?

Planning and organising

(Thinking ahead for self and others.)

- Have you set your own revision timetable for different subjects?
- Are you involved in organising events: school prom or charity days? Youth centre events? Through your voluntary work?

Problem-solving

(Thinking about things in different ways and providing creative solutions.)

- Are you taking GCSEs, Standard grades or other qualifications in any practical problem-solving subjects (particularly ICT, engineering, DT or any of the applied subjects)?
- Are you involved in Young Enterprise or Young Engineer activities?

■ Have you been involved in team-building days through school or elsewhere?

Research skills

(Knowing where to look for information.)

■ Do you have to know where to look things up for assignments and coursework?

■ Do you have to decide which is the best source of information? (Not always the internet!)

■ Did your work experience involve doing any research for the employer, such as compiling lists of contacts for marketing campaigns?

Teamwork

(Working alongside and co-operating with other people.)

The most obvious example is a sports team, but you don't need to be involved in sports to find examples of teamwork skills.

■ Have you been involved in group projects where success depends on everyone working together: performing arts productions, school events?

■ Have you done outdoor activities where you have relied on other members of the team and they have relied on you for success: and, in some cases, for their safety?

■ Have you undertaken expeditions for your DofE or as part of a course, where you have had to work together to get each other through a gruelling situation?

■ Were you part of any team tasks in your work experience?

■ Do you work as part of a team in a part-time job or as a volunteer, where each of you relies on everyone else's performance for the team's success?

■ Are you in a band or orchestra? (Whether this is organised by school or by you and some friends, it still relies on teamwork for success.)

Can you see how the activities which form part of your everyday life – getting to school or college, completing your work on time, fitting in a part-time job, being involved in sports or other activities, pursuing your hobbies and interests – involve these all-important transferable skills?

TIP If you are managing to fit all your activities into your busy life – and do well at all of them – you have plenty of transferable skills.

Getting it into your CV

You need to be very clear to employers to make sure they realise that you have these skills – don't leave it to the person reading your CV to work it out. They won't. You need to point it out to them.

Which activities for me?

You will notice that certain activities have been mentioned several times in this book, for example working as a group on projects such as Young Enterprise, DofE or ASDAN. As well as being enjoyable to take part in – the main reason why anyone gets involved! – they help you develop many of the skills that employers look for.

For this reason, employers often look for these activities on the young people's CVs. It's not quite as simple as 'if you do Young Enterprise, DofE or ASDAN you'll get a job', but taking part in those sorts of activities is likely to help you attract the attention of employers as they read your CV.

A word of warning

It really isn't worth doing any activity just because:

- 'it'll help me get a job'

or

■ 'it looks good on my CV'.

It's only worth getting involved in something if it genuinely interests you. If you become involved in any activity, in or out of school, that you don't really enjoy you are likely to find yourself quickly losing interest and therefore not wanting to put in the commitment that these activities demand. And remember, too, that your CV is your route to getting an interview. If an employer asks you about any of the activities on your CV, you want to be able to talk about it enthusiastically and sound keen. That won't work if you are doing something you don't really enjoy.

TIP The best activities to choose to develop your skills are the ones you enjoy.

What do you know now?

■ Employers are interested in your transferable skills.
■ You are using these skills on a daily basis.
■ You will need to tell employers which skills your activities demonstrate.

9 PLUGGING THE GAP

I stressed in Chapter 7 that there is no need to lie on your CV. But what do you do if you haven't got what's needed to apply for a job (or other opportunity)?

The easy answer is that if something's missing from your CV, you have to go out and get it! But, like a lot else in life, that can be easier said than done. It's not impossible, though. It might take a bit of creative thinking to work out which activity will get you what you need – probably followed by a lot of persistence to get where you want to be.

Whether or not this applies to you might depend on how far you have got with thinking about your future and your career.

Career choices

As you read this book, you will be making decisions about your future or, at least, starting to think about your career options. As you will know from your friends and peers, people differ in how clear they are about their future plans. Some people seem very certain from an early age which career they want to follow, while others remain undecided for a long time. In fact, a large number of young people leave school, college or even university without a clear idea of where they want to go in life. (And some adults, even at quite a late stage in their working life, claim not to know what they 'really want to do'!)

At this stage one of the following may apply to you.

- **You know the career you want to follow**
  Perhaps you have made up your mind about a future career. If you've discussed it with other people – careers

teacher, careers/personal adviser, subject teachers, parents or carers and other interested people – you may know about the usual entry routes and what you need to get there, in terms of qualifications and experience.

■ **You have some general career ideas**
Maybe you know which broad area you want to go into but you're not certain exactly which career you would like to aim at. You're still looking at the options in a whole career area, such as health and social care, creative arts or science, for example. You may be starting to find out what sort of skills, attributes, qualifications and experience are relevant.

■ **You're still thinking about a career plan: and keeping your options open**
Perhaps you're forming an idea about what you don't want to do in the future, which can be just as important at this stage.

If you know which career you want to pursue you are probably already working hard at school to get the right qualifications.

The right experience

What are these gaps in your CV that you might need to fill? They're most likely to involve experience relevant to a career area. Sometimes it's possible to get the right experience from part-time work. If you want a career in retail, for example, there are plenty of places to look for a job which will give you relevant experience. If you want to work with motor vehicles, you could look for work valeting cars, in a parts supplier or in a car accessories retailer.

If you can't manage to get a relevant paid job you need to look for experience in other ways. And, of course, there is a whole range of jobs where you'd be unlikely to be able to get a paid part-time job anyway. If you are thinking about becoming a doctor or other healthcare professional, for example, or work in manufacturing in a factory environment, it would be hard to get real paid work.

In some of these occupations, it may still be worth looking for paid work that is related in some way to your chosen career. If you wanted to be social worker, for example, work in a residential home would be useful; if you plan to become a vet, dog walking or pet sitting would be relevant; or for working in law (as a solicitor or barrister, maybe) office administration at a branch of a local law firm might help.

In order to get some direct experience or a real taste of what the work involves, you may have to do:

- work experience
- work shadowing
- voluntary work
- an internship.

There are some career choices which require work experience, shadowing or volunteering before your application will be considered. This is mainly because you have to be sure that you know what the work involves before you start applying for jobs or courses. Examples include:

- agriculture
- social work
- teaching
- medicine
- dentistry
- veterinary work
- healthcare professions, such as physiotherapy and occupational therapy.

Some of these occupations are also very popular and there is a high demand for both jobs and places on courses, training schemes and apprenticeships. Taking the trouble to arrange some work experience or shadowing shows you are keen and really committed to the work. Anything that demonstrates your enthusiasm will help your application.

Other fields that have become very popular and therefore hard to get into include:

- the media
- fashion
- advertising
- environmental work
- the arts
- cultural heritage, including museum and art gallery work.

Many people spend a long time working on a voluntary basis before they get their first paid job in these areas.

Work experience

Your school may encourage or arrange work experience, often in Year 10 or 11 (S3 or S4). Depending on which courses you are taking, there may be other opportunities: work experience is now part of many courses, including 14–19 Diplomas, the Welsh Baccalaureate and vocational courses such as NVQs. Other courses, such as the AQA Baccalaureate, offer it as an enrichment option.

Some schools organise work experience placements, but there is usually the option of organising your own. In college, you are more likely to play a greater part in choosing and arranging a placement, and sometimes the process of selecting, finding and applying for work experience is part of the course.

Whether you or your school or college arranges the work experience is sometimes a matter of who has the contacts.

Over time, your teachers or tutors will have built up contacts with local organisations who are happy to have young people in their workplaces and know what sort of experiences young people want to gain from being there. Colleges too will often have contacts in their vocational area, or at least be able to give you some pointers about where to start looking.

You might be lucky enough to know someone who works in the career area you are interested in who is happy to have you in their organisation.

School work experience is usually one week or two and, generally, the whole year group (or course group) goes out on work experience at the same time. Beyond school, work experience can be a different arrangement – sometimes blocks of several weeks or perhaps one day a week over a term.

But the term 'work experience' can describe any short-term unpaid time spent in the workplace. If you arrange to spend a week of the holidays in someone's office, garage, studio or library, that is also work experience. Whatever the arrangement, an employer will see this as equally valid when s/he reads it on your CV.

Work shadowing

'Work experience' carries with it the idea that you have taken part in the work and been given some tasks to do. This is not always possible – you couldn't perform a surgical procedure, speak in a court case, operate a chainsaw, manufacture chemicals or colour someone's hair on a work experience placement.

In situations like this, you'd have to do the next best thing – which is work shadowing. This means spending time with someone as they go about their work. You watch what they're doing and they explain things as they go along.

Work shadowing might be for a day or longer.

Voluntary work

This can be a good way to explore a career which you like the sound of as well as getting valuable experience to add to your CV, to make you more interesting to an employer.

'Voluntary' means you are not getting paid, but if the work gives you the experience you need to get into your chosen career it will be worth the effort. Voluntary organisations appreciate that people are giving up their own time and you can be very clear about how much time you can spare – a regular evening each week or an afternoon each month, perhaps, or a day every now and then, by agreement.

Many voluntary organisations will pay expenses. This means they are likely to pay your fares. Even though you are not being paid, you shouldn't end up out of pocket.

Don't worry that 'voluntary work doesn't count'. It does. In many cases, the work you do as a volunteer is similar to or exactly the same as a paid job. For example, charity shop volunteers provide customer service, organise the stock and handle money in the same way as in any other retail outlet.

Some voluntary work will give you the chance to take responsibility that you might not get at the same age in a paid job. For example, if you are a leader with the Guide or Scout Association you could be organising activities for groups of Beavers or Cubs, Rainbows or Brownies. (Of course, you will not be expected to take on responsibility unless you are ready and willing to do so.) If you are planning a career as a teacher or youth worker this would be very valuable experience, both for your own self-confidence and to show an employer on your CV. Even if you do not intend to work with young people, the level of responsibility and the organisational skills you are using will impress an employer.

In some cases, voluntary work is the only way to get the right experience. You are unlikely to be able to get your first job in an environmental career or as an art historian without having worked as a volunteer.

Like a job, though, voluntary work is a commitment. Voluntary organisations rely on their volunteers. If you don't turn up when you've said you will, you are letting someone down. Commitment is important for your CV; your commitment will interest an employer as much as the nature of the voluntary work. The employer will know you are someone who can be relied on.

Voluntary work may have the advantage over paid work of being more easily available. Instead of competing with lots of other people for a paid job, you may find that a voluntary organisation welcomes you.

Internships

This is a relatively new term for a period of unpaid work for an organisation. Some large organisations now have well-developed internship programmes with an application process and strict closing dates. It is important to realise, though, that the word can be used to describe different placements, some of which only apply to those who are already at university.

Some internships are paid; others are unpaid. What distinguishes an internship from any other kind of work experience placement is that they are usually for a longer, fixed period – often six months or a year.

Using your CV to support your career plans

If you apply for work experience, work shadowing, voluntary work or an internship, you are likely to be making a speculative application. Some voluntary organisations advertise vacancies and there are annual programmes of internships with their own application process, but on the whole you will be applying to an organisation 'on the off-chance'.

This means you will be trying even harder to attract the employer's attention. If they haven't advertised a vacancy, they are probably not looking for staff. In any case, organisations don't really look for people on work experience. If they take you on for a placement they are doing you a favour.

So when you use your CV to ask an employer for a placement, you need to tell them very clearly:

- what you are asking the employer for
- what your career ambitions are
- why they should give you the placement.

Here's an example. Kirsty wants a career teaching art to children with special needs As you can see from her CV, she has some relevant experience in her summer jobs and her work experience placement. She wants to add to her skills in the art and design world by becoming a volunteer at an art gallery in a nearby town.

Kirsty McBride
10 Home Road
Mytown FR1 2PQ
01323 456789 email: kirstymcb@anymail.co.uk

Profile
Sixth-form student with creative design skills. I am involved in the school centenary art project and have led art workshops at a special needs summer play scheme. I am looking for voluntary work to further the skills and experience I have gained.

Qualifications
St Peter's School, Anytown

GCSEs	English	A
	French	A
	Art	A
	ICT	B
	Maths	C
	Science	C
AS level	English	B
A level	English	(to be completed summer 2011)
BTEC	Art and Design	(to be completed summer 2011)

CAD level 2

Skills and Achievements
- Customer service skills in busy supermarket at weekends
- Designed a direct mail leaflet for local company while on work experience
- Organised the design of the sixth-form centenary mural
- Leading art workshops with special needs children

Experience
Supersaver store 2008 – present
Weekend job at Supersaver store including customer service, till duties, shelf stacking and displays. Working overtime where necessary.

Playdays Play Scheme July–August 2010
Assistant Leader of special needs summer play scheme, helping to organise the schedule as well as leading workshops.

Playdays Play Scheme July–August 2009
Assistant at special needs summer play scheme, leading art sessions.

ABC Design May 2007
2 weeks' work experience including production, design and marketing departments.

Interests
Visiting art galleries, particularly new touring exhibitions

References available on request

Her personal profile is a good start. She has told the reader:

- what she has done – by summarising her CV
- what she is looking for – a voluntary role.

However, when Kirsty looked at her CV again she realised she could have been clearer about what she wanted and why. She decided to rewrite her personal profile.

> **Profile**
> Sixth-form student with creative design skills. I am involved
> in the school centenary art project and have led art
> workshops at a special needs summer play scheme.
> I would like to become a volunteer gallery assistant to
> gain further experience for a career teaching art to
> children with special needs.

It is now much clearer to the reader what Kirsty is asking them for and how it fits in with her career plans.

Another example. This time Ashley is seeking work experience at a local accountants' firm.

> **Profile**
> I am seeking a work experience placement as part of my
> Diploma in Business and Administration and Finance. I am
> keen to pursue a career in accountancy. I am involved in
> Young Enterprise and charity fundraising at my Youth Hub.

Ashley states clearly what he wants.

Sending your request

Part of making a request for work experience, work shadowing, voluntary work or an internship is getting that request to the right person. It is worth doing some research to get this right.

You could send your CV in to the organisation by addressing it to the company name or using a likely department name or job title – HR Department, HR Director, Head of Personnel, Training Manager, etc. But remember that you are making a request to the company, rather than applying for an advertised vacancy, so it is up to you to make the effort to find out who to send it to.

You could find out:

- on the internet: some company websites have names (and profiles) of senior staff
- by phoning the organisation
- by calling in and asking.

It is also important to include a covering letter. You can use this to give more information about your request and yourself.

Kirsty's letter is shown on the next page.

10 Home Road
Mytown
FR1 2PQ
01234 98765

Ms A Saunders
Volunteer Manager
The Gallery
Town Square
Our Town
AY10 2PQ

18th September 2011

Dear Ms Saunders

Volunteer Gallery Assistant
I would like to apply to join your volunteer programme as an assistant.

I am interested in becoming a teacher of art to children with special needs. I have spent two summers working at a special needs play scheme. I am also involved in art projects at school.

I spend time visiting art exhibitions, including those at The Gallery. I particularly enjoyed the 20th-Century Graphics exhibition. Working as volunteer would increase my knowledge of the art world.

I am available on Sundays and some weekday evenings

Yours sincerely

KIRSTY McBRIDE

Chapter 11 has more information about covering letters.

What do you know now?

■ You can target organisations which will give the experience you need.

■ You may have to work as a volunteer to get the right experience.

■ If an organisation takes you on for work experience they are doing you a favour.

10 HORSES FOR COURSES

Chapter 8 looked at the skills that employers are looking for and Chapter 9 looked at some of the ways you could get the right experience.

Now it's time to look at how to target your CV to a particular vacancy. This is known as tailoring your CV. This means that you put in the information which is particularly relevant to that vacancy – information which will signal to the employer that you are (or might be) the person they are looking for to fill the vacancy.

Personal profile

We've already established that you are almost certainly going to have four to six lines (three or four sentences) forming some kind of personal statement at, or near, the top of your CV. Why do most CVs include this?

- ■ It's become a convention.
- ■ Employers expect it.
- ■ It's your chance to personalise your CV.
- ■ Why not? (What would you put there instead?)

What's in a name?

I have seen this section of the CV called all these things.

- ■ Introduction
- ■ Personal Profile
- ■ Profile

- Personal Statement
- Personal Summary
- Statement
- Summary
- Summary Statement

Less commonly, I've also seen these.

- About Me
- Candidate Profile

The most commonly used terms for this section, though, is 'Personal Profile', with 'Profile' coming a close second. (In this chapter, I'm going to use the term 'Personal Profile'.)

Of course, there is an alternative.

Call it nothing at all – just write it. If you're agonising about what to call this section, think again. Does it need a title at all? Don't worry, you'll be in good company: I've probably seen as many CVs with no title for this section as with a title. This really is one of those optional points.

So, you decide!

What is less of an option, though, is whether or not to have a profile. Like any other section of a good CV, it's there for a purpose.

Personal statement?

At this point, I want to avoid any possible confusion between a UCAS (Universities and Colleges Admissions Service) personal statement and the personal profile section of your CV. They are **not the same thing**!

If you're applying to university yourself, or you know people who are applying, you will have heard about 'personal statements' for the UCAS form. You just need to be aware that the personal profile section of your CV is completely different from the UCAS personal statement. The only similarity is that they form part of an application and therefore each is trying to attract the attention of the reader and interest them in the person applying. But that's where the similarity ends – UCAS personal statements and CV personal profiles differ in what they say, how they say it, how long they are and in what they are trying to do.

What's the personal profile for?

A well-written, appropriate personal profile is intended to do any one or more of these:

- catch the reader's attention
- act as an introduction to your CV
- highlight the important parts of your CV
- summarise your CV
- tell the reader what is unique about you
- point out to the reader why you are suitable for the job.

An effective, attractive personal profile does *all* those things! And all in a few sentences – that's asking a lot. A few sentences, you may be thinking – it's beginning to sound more like an essay. But an essay is exactly what it mustn't be. You are aiming to attract the reader's attention, not drown them in a sea of words.

Do your research

In order to tailor your CV to show how you are suitable for a particular vacancy, you need to find out as much as you can about the vacancy and about the organisation.

The first place to look is the job ad itself. Sometimes the employer specifies what they are looking for.

Busy supermarket has ongoing vacancies for Till staff
and
Shelf stackers

Must be able to work weekends
and
Have customer service experience

Send or bring your CV to

The Manager
Busystores
Main Road
Our Town
AY3 5XY

This employer is asking all applicants to meet certain conditions.

- They must be able to work weekends.
- They must have experience of customer service.

To be of interest to the employer, anyone who applies for the job not only has to be able to meet these specifications, but has to show clearly that they do.

You will need to specify somewhere on your CV that you are available and willing to work at weekends. It's no good thinking to yourself, 'The employer will know that I can do weekends or

I wouldn't have applied.' That's too risky. The employer may think that – or they may think 'This applicant hasn't mentioned anything about weekends. Perhaps she didn't notice that on my ad. Never mind, I've dozens of other applications, I don't need this one.'

In addition, you will need to point out all your customer service experience. Remember that customer service doesn't have to be in a retail store – it could be on a school charity stall, for example. It doesn't even have to involve buying and selling – what about when you showed prospective parents around your school on an Open Evening or when you took your turn on the message desk running errands for school staff?

To tie your different experiences together and bring them to the attention of the employer, it is worth summarising them in your personal profile. You might want to do it like this.

Lee Brookman
23 The Place
Ourtown
AY9 4XT
01234 98765 07875 123456
leebrookman@mymail.com

Personal profile
I have a range of customer service experience dealing with adults and peers including stalls at school charity fairs, school open events and the college Freshers' Fair. I am keen to add to my retail experience with a weekend job.

Some employers do not tell you much in their ad.

What other detail could you give that might attract the employer? There are some clues in the ad. The coffee shop is described as 'busy' so the employer is likely to be interested in any other busy environments you have worked in.

Assistant Wanted

Saturday assistant wanted
For busy high street coffee shop

Send a CV to:
The Manager
That Café
High Street
Our Town
AY10 2PQ

Closing date: 12th August

Then you would need to think about what else might attract an employer. What other skills and experience would be relevant for a café? What about:

- catering or food preparation experience, including food tech at school or food hygiene at school or elsewhere
- customer service: again this could be from any activity that has involved dealing with people.

This employer has not specified any requirements, such as experience of similar work. However, the job is described as 'Saturday assistant', so it would be worth mentioning that you are available on Saturdays.

Beyond the advertisement

Employers will like to see that you have made some effort to find out about their company. If you really want to make sure your CV is relevant and attractive to the employer, you can look further than the employer's ad.

You could, for example, have a look at the organisation's website – most places have them nowadays. From a website you might find out:

- what the organisation does
- how long it's been in business
- how big it is
- whether it's part of a larger organisation
- how successful it is
- who works there.

You might not use all that information to tailor your CV, but it will help you build up a picture of the place you are applying to work. Even if it doesn't seem directly relevant at this stage, the more you know about a company when you apply for a job there, the better.

TIP Any research you do about an organisation is also useful preparation for an interview.

For example, if you find out whether the company you are applying to has a few local branches or is a large national – or even international – company, you could refer to this in your personal profile. Lee, for instance, could have added:

> **Personal profile**
> I have a range of customer service experience dealing with adults and peers including stalls at school charity fairs, school open events and the college Freshers' Fair. I am keen to add to my retail experience with a weekend job in a well-established local company.

It always helps to say something flattering about the organisation, especially if that's what they say about themselves on their website. We all like to hear other people say good things about us (or to us), and employers are no different. All companies like to think of themselves as having a good reputation and they will be pleased to hear that you agree.

These are some examples of words and phrases you might see companies using about themselves:

- good reputation
- high standards
- highly regarded
- leading
- long established
- well established
- well thought of.

Other applications

The same goes for work experience, work shadowing, internships and voluntary work. You can tailor your application by doing some research to find out more about the organisation. Then you will be able to make it clear to the employer why you have chosen that organisation.

For example, Grant is hoping to do his work experience in a gym. To increase his chances of finding the work experience he wants, he is sending his CV to several different companies. For each application, he has set out clearly his qualifications, the sports he is involved with and the teams he plays for. Rather than just send the same CV to each employer, he has decided to use his personal profile to tailor his approach to the companies.

First, a nearby branch of a national chain of leisure clubs:

> **Personal profile**
> I am a keen sportsman and member of school teams as well as a local rugby club. I would like to spend two weeks' work experience in the Mytown Club. I am planning a career in sports and leisure management and spending time with a well-known national chain of gyms would give me a valuable insight into the industry.

Next, a local independent gym:

> **Personal profile**
> I am a keen sportsman and member of school teams as well as a local rugby club. I would like to spend two weeks' work experience in the Mytown Club. I am planning a career in sports and leisure management and spending time at a local independent gym with a good reputation would give me a valuable insight into the industry.

And finally, the gym where he is a member:

> **Personal profile**
> I am a keen sportsman and member of school teams as well as a local rugby club. I would like to spend two weeks' work experience in the Mytown Club. I am planning a career in sports and leisure management and spending time at a gym I know well and which sets high standards would give me a valuable insight into the industry.

As you can see, Grant did not completely change the wording of each personal profile – he just changed enough for the employer reading his CV to realise that Grant knows a bit about the company and has thought about why he's applying to them.

Inside information

It's not just websites which will give you information about an organisation you are applying to. You can learn a lot from paying a visit to the place, if that's possible. There will, of course be plenty of workplaces where you cannot do this. There's no point in trying to visit a factory, office, workshop or hospital. But if you are applying to a shop, café, leisure centre or garage, for example, you could take a look.

What could you find out from a visit?

- How busy the business is. (Try visiting at different times of day.)
- Who the customers are.
- What products they provide.
- Whether there's a staff uniform or dress code.
- How staff talk and act to each other.
- How the staff treat the customers.
- What hours they are open.

> ### Personal profile
> I have a range of customer service experience dealing with adults and peers including stalls at school charity fairs, school open events and the college Freshers' Fair. I am keen to add to my retail experience with a weekend job in a well-established local company selling high fashion menswear.

Even if it's somewhere you have been a customer in the past, it's still worth a visit in person. You might find yourself looking at the company differently if you think you might work there.

> ### Personal profile
> I have a range of customer service experience dealing with adults and peers including stalls at school charity fairs, school open events and the college Freshers' Fair. I am keen to add to my retail experience with a weekend job in a high fashion shop where I am a regular customer.

Of course, this mainly applies if your application is to a local organisation or local branch of a national organisation. But if you were applying for a job, or training scheme, on a national basis, it would still be worth looking at your local branch.

Personal profile

I have a range of customer service experience dealing with adults and peers including stalls at school charity fairs, school open events and the college Freshers' Fair. A company with an emphasis on customer service and a range of high-quality DIY products would be an ideal start to my chosen career in retail management.

There is another way you can find out about the organisation you are applying to. Do you know anyone else who works there? This could help you get real inside information.

Be professional

It's true that you want to stand out from the crowd and show the employer why you are different from the other applicants and therefore suitable for the job but you want to make an impression on the employer for the right reasons. It is important to come across as:

- professional
- businesslike
- smart
- someone the employer would like to have working for them.

It's fine to be interesting, but you need to be interesting for the right reasons. You will interest the employer by having the right qualifications and experience to match their requirements and by showing that you have the right qualities and skills for the job.

You attract the employer's attention by making your CV

- professional
- businesslike
- smart

so that you look like

- someone the employer would like to have working for them.

Chapter 6 covered the points about presentation and Chapter 11 will look at sending off of your CV to employers – all in a professional, businesslike way.

TIP Fancy fonts, patterned paper or colour printing are more likely to put off or annoy an employer than impress them.

You may have heard or read about people who try to make their CV really stand out, perhaps by adding pictures or other designs, printing it on a T shirt – and wearing it – or creating a leaflet. Most employers will not be interested in receiving a CV like this. With most employers an approach like this is more likely to harm your chances of success. It would be taking quite a big risk.

That may not put you off. You may want to take the risk. If you are very creative and feel you have a good idea to approach the right employer with, go for it! However, you may want to bear in mind that these approaches to catching an employer's attention can only succeed if they are true one-offs. As soon as lots of people do unusual things they stop being unusual and lose their effect.

Particularly as you progress along your chosen career path, there are some specialist areas which demand a bit more than a standard CV. For example:

- for performing arts you will need a show reel of your performances
- for computer gaming you will need a demo disk with examples of games you've coded and modifications you've worked on
- for CAD (computer-aided design) work you will need to show your designs
- for art and design you will need a portfolio of your work.

Entry into these areas is very competitive. To enter one of these highly competitive fields you will need support from someone who is already a specialist in the field – probably your teacher or tutor.

This book is about the general approach to CVs for more conventional jobs.

What do you know now?

- You can use the personal profile to tailor your CV to a particular vacancy.
- Employers will be impressed if you have found out about their organisation.
- CVs need to be professional and businesslike.

11 OK, I'VE WRITTEN IT: WHAT NEXT?

Phew! You've finally got your CV as you want it. It looks good and it says all the right things about you. What now?

Check it and proofread it.

Wait a minute – we did that in Chapter 6, didn't we? Can I suggest you do it once more . . .

. . . and then, to be on the safe side, look through it again.

That's how important it is to get it right. You don't want any mistakes if you're sending your CV to an employer. The vacancy you're applying for is an important step in your career path and you don't want to do anything that might spoil your chances before you've even started.

As described in Chapter 6, you might also want to check again how your CV looks when you print it, and when it's emailed, especially if you've made a lot of changes to it after reading some of the other chapters.

Get a second opinion

I've said all along that it's your CV, that it's important that you write it yourself and that you need to be happy with its style and content. However, none of this stops you asking other people's opinions. As we said in Chapter 1, you are likely to know a variety of people who are willing to help you through this stage. One of the ways they can help is by looking through your CV with a constructively critical eye. Maybe you would value the opinion of, for example:

- family or family friends and contacts
- teachers or tutors
- your friends or other peers
- anyone else you know whose opinion you value.

And again, as I said in Chapter 1, you can ask other people for their opinions and listen to what they have to say, but you can use your own judgement to decide what you are going to take on board.

Sending off your CV

Remember those job ads from Chapter 2?

Assistant Wanted

Saturday assistant wanted
For busy high street coffee shop

Send a CV to:
The Manager
That Café
High Street
Our Town
AY10 2PQ

Closing date: 12 August

Staff Wanted

For new sports shop opening in September

Full-time and part-time staff wanted

Email your CV to

APerson@anemail.com

By 12 August

**Busy supermarket has on-going vacancies for Till staff
and
Shelf stackers**

Must be able to work weekends
and
Have customer service experience

Send or bring your CV to

The Manager
Busystores
Main Road
Our Town
AY3 5XY

Each of them asks for a CV, but asks you to submit it in a different way.

Printing your CV

If the employer is asking you to send or bring your CV, they obviously want to see a hard copy. If you're sending your CV to an employer you want it to look smart, so use reasonable quality paper. Usually you'll use white (that's what most people have in their printers anyway). Some people use off-white or cream-coloured paper – that's OK too. But you don't need to go and buy non-white paper specially. Nor do you need to buy expensive, heavy-quality paper. You might read (or be told) that CVs need to be printed on 'top-quality paper'. But usual printer-quality paper is fine.

Here's another of those CV 'rules'.

No coloured paper.

CVs are not the place for coloured paper. Remember, you are aiming to look businesslike and business documents are printed on white paper.

Similarly, don't print the text in any colour except black.

Do what the employer wants

It's very important, when applying for jobs, that you do what the employer asks. Even if you don't agree with it, you still need to follow the instructions. You may think it's slow and old-fashioned to send a CV through the post – emailing it would be much quicker and would save you printing it. All that may be true, but if it's not what the employer is asking then, on this occasion, it doesn't matter.

Some employers give you a choice, like the Busystores super-market ad above. If this is the case, it is a genuine choice.

You will not have any more chance of being successful in your application if you send your CV than if you take it in (or the other way round).

Emailing your CV

If the employer asks you to email your CV, that's what you do. It would be very unusual for them to ask you to email your CV without clearly giving you an email address. There may be more than one address mentioned in the advertisement or in the application details elsewhere. So check before you send it that you're using the right email address.

Think carefully too about what you will put in the 'Subject' line of your email. Don't leave it blank – the employer may get hundreds of emails on different subjects each day. You want to be absolutely sure that your application gets there – and goes to the right person.

What would it make sense to put in that subject line? Something that identifies what you are sending. Sometimes the employer asks you to use a particular subject line, such as 'New Staff' or 'Recruitment', perhaps. Or there may be a reference number for the job vacancy. Even if the employer doesn't ask you to use the reference number it's a good idea. So your email might start like this:

> To: recruitment@jonesbrothers.co.uk
> Subject: Ref: 594/10 Application for office assistant post

It's usual to send a CV as an attachment. Don't be tempted to copy and paste the text into the email itself. There are several reasons for this.

- All your careful formatting and page layout is likely to become distorted.
- The employer will want to print copies of your CV

when it arrives – it's much easier to do this from an attachment.

■ They may want to save your CV to a Word folder (probably with all the other CVs they receive). Again this is easier for the employer if your CV is a separate Word document.

TIP Rather than just attaching the CV, it's polite to write something in your email saying you have attached it.

A short note might do. Perhaps:

> To: recruitment@jonesbrothers.co.uk
> Subject: Ref: 594/10 Application for office assistant post
>
> Dear Sir
> I would like to apply for the post of office assistant advertised in the *Weekly News*.
> I am attaching my CV.
>
> Sunita Devi

(You can if you like, and if you're feeling confident, write a bit more. The section dealing with covering letters, below, can also be applied to emails.)

Then make sure you remember to attach your CV!

It might be worth thinking about what you call the attachment, too. If you've been working on your CV for a while, you might have several versions. As you work on your PC, you've probably given these versions different file names. By the time you get to the stage when you've got your CV how you want it, the file name might be called something like 'myCV[5]'.

If you just attach that to your email, that's how the employer will receive it. 'myCV[5]' the employer might think – that's an unusual name. When you email your CV to the employer, it will look much more professional if you name the file using your name. For example: 'mynameCV' or 'mynameCVjuly2011'. (Make sure that you use the current date – you don't want to give the employer the impression that your CV's out of date.)

Closing dates

Whichever method the employer wants you to use to submit your CV, you must get it there by the closing date. You will see that two of the ads above give a closing date for applications. This is just as important as following any of the other instructions in a job advertisement. It cannot be stressed enough that the closing date is a *deadline*.

You are used to deadlines for homework and, even more important, for coursework. You know that there's trouble if you don't meet the deadline, especially for dates set externally by examining bodies to submit course work for GCSEs and other public exams.

TIP Closing dates for job vacancies (or any other sort of application) need to be treated as immovable.

Some closing dates also give a time – often by 5 p.m. (the end of the working day). Some may say 12 noon or possibly by 10 a.m. Giving a time is much more common if the employer is asking for CVs to be emailed rather than sent in. (You, as the sender, have much more control over the time an email arrives than you do over what time a letter arrives in the post.) Again, this is an important part of the application process and you need to meet any time deadlines as well as dates.

Think about it. You are applying for a job with that employer. If you are successful you will be part of the staff team. The people who recruited you – looked through your CV and, perhaps, interviewed you – will be your colleagues. You may be working with them every day. You want to get off on the right footing with them, as someone who can follow a simple instruction and get things done on time, in the way you are asked to do it. It's better to get things right from the start.

It's a good idea to send or email your application well before the closing date (or time) to give yourself a margin for error.

By the way, this is not just the employer setting tasks for the applicants or making you jump through unnecessary hoops. Once the applications are in the employer's office, that's when their work starts. They need to look through the applications. There may be all sorts of reasons why they need to get the process done at a particular time or within a certain timeframe.

But, you're thinking, the ad for Busystores supermarket doesn't give a closing date. What do I do there? In this case, the ad says 'ongoing vacancies'. This means instead of having one recruitment drive at a particular time (for one vacancy, or for several), as some employers do, this employer recruits more or less all the time. This is likely to be because vacancies arise from time to time on a pretty regular basis. So it's safe to send in your CV when you're ready: but it also makes sense not to wait too long. Remember, you won't be the only person who wants to apply to Busystores.

Occasionally, it may be the case that there is no closing date mentioned and the advertisement doesn't say that recruitment is ongoing. This could be because, for example:

■ the employer forgot to put the date in the ad
■ the newspaper forgot to print the date.

Mistakes do happen – even employers are human.

TIP If you are in any doubt about the closing date, it's perfectly OK to phone the employer and ask. Better to be sure than miss that all-important closing date.

Sending your CV

It's worth taking a bit of time over how you send your CV. If at all possible, use a large envelope so you don't have to fold your CV. You want it to look as good as possible when it arrives at the employers.

And, of course, you have to be sure you address the envelope clearly – using the correct, and full, address. If the ad says to send your CV to a particular person or department, make sure that's clear above the address too.

Enclosures

That means anything that goes in (is enclosed) with your CV in the envelope. Again, check whether the employer is asking you to send anything else with your CV – copies of your certificates or a photo, maybe. As I've said before, your application won't get very far if you don't follow the employer's instructions.

There is one enclosure which you need to send with your CV – some sort of covering letter.

Covering letters

Just think about this scenario: a CV arrives through the post and is put on the manager's desk in the Ourtown branch of Busystores. There's nothing else in the envelope. The manager has a quick glance at the CV. It looks interesting – the applicant has some customer service experience. But which job are they applying for – shelf stacker or till assistant? The manager's having a busy day, as usual, the phone's ringing and she needs to get out onto the shop floor. There's no time to wonder which pile to put the CV into, so I'm afraid it goes in the bin.

What a waste, if you've spent a long time preparing your CV and making it relevant for the job you want. That's why a CV should always have a covering letter with it.

Perhaps you don't write letters very often. Business letters have quite a standard format.

Your address
Your telephone number
(including area code)

Date in full

Position and address of the
person you are writing to

Dear Sir/Madam or Mr/Ms _____

Subject of letter
Contents

Yours faithfully/sincerely

Signature

FULL NAME IN CAPITALS

TIP If at all possible, try to find out the name of a person you can address your covering letter to. You may find a name in the advertisement or in the application details.

If the ad just says 'The Manager' or 'The HR Department', don't start your letter 'Dear Manager' (and certainly not 'Dear HR Department')

You could try phoning the employer to find out. If you can't find out a name it'll have to be 'Dear Sir' or 'Dear Sir/Madam'.

How to end a letter

The official, businesslike way to do it is:

- ■ 'Yours sincerely' if you are using someone's name
- ■ 'Yours faithfully' if you start with Dear Sir or Madam.

16 The Street
Mytown
PN2 4FG
01234 98765

10th September 2011

The Manager
That Café
High Street
Our Town
AY10 2PQ

Dear Sir

I would like to apply for the post of Saturday assistant. I am enclosing my CV.

Yours faithfully

SUNITA DEVI

This is a very short letter but it does what it needs to do and would be fine to send as it is. However, if you want to, you can use your covering letter to say a bit more about yourself:

16 The Street
Mytown
PN2 4FG
01234 98765

10th September 2011

The Manager
That Café
High Street
Our Town
AY10 2PQ

Dear Sir

Saturday assistant
I would like to apply for the post of Saturday assistant.
I am enclosing my CV.

As you can see, last summer I worked in a high street
fast food outlet and am used to working hard in a busy
environment.

I could attend an interview on a Saturday or after school.

Yours faithfully

SUNITA DEVI

Sunita's experience in the fast food outlet is on her CV but, knowing that it is relevant for the job, she has used the covering letter to draw the employer's attention to it.

Like your CV, your covering letter needs to be typed and printed. (The only exception to this is where the employer has specifically asked for a handwritten covering letter. Occasionally an employer does this to get an idea of how neat the applicant is.)

TIP It's a good idea to paperclip your letter to your CV – you don't want one or other to go astray – but staples are a nuisance if the employer wants to photocopy the CV.

Remember to sign the letter!

Handing in your CV

If that's one of the options offered by the employer, you may prefer to hand in your CV personally. It's still a good idea to put it in an envelope, to keep it neat. The person you hand it to may not be the person the applications have to go to. If it's a large organisation, for example, you may hand it in at a reception desk. In a smaller organisation, the manager may be available or may have asked the shop floor staff to put the applications to one side. Either way, you need to address the envelope in the same way you would if you were sending in your application.

Uploading your CV

This is another method of submitting a CV and it is becoming more and more common as more employers recruit over the internet. Uploading a CV is easy to do – you may already have done it. The site allows you to browse your files to locate your CV. What happens next varies slightly from site to site.

- On some sites your CV is copied and pasted into a box on the recruitment site.
- On others it is sent as an attachment.

If you are copying and pasting your CV, you will get a chance to look at it before you press the 'submit' button; otherwise you submit it without a chance to see it.

TIP If you're uploading your CV it's important to check it carefully before you upload and send it to make sure, for example, that you are using the correct, most up-to-date version.

What you will notice, if you are copying and pasting your CV into a website like this, is that your CV looks a bit different from the original Word version. For example:

- bullets may have changed, moved or been removed
- centred text (such as your contact details) may be reformatted or distorted
- other attributes, such as bold or underline, or any special characters may have been removed.

Your CV, therefore, may not look quite as you want it to look for an employer. All your careful work getting the right layout seems to be wasted. It is worth having a 'plain' version of your CV for uploading. Basic CV format 1 in Chapter 5 might be a good one to use as a basis for this.

Has it arrived?

Your CV's gone off safely to the employer. At least, that's what you hope. If you've handed in your CV you know it got there OK, but if you sent it by post or email, how do you know it's arrived safely? You don't unless you check.

It can be easier to check that your CV has arrived by email than by post. Some email systems will allow you to 'request a receipt' (but remember the person receiving the email can decide not to send the receipt). You could add a simple request to the email you send with your CV.

To: recruitment@jonesbrothers.co.uk
Subject: Ref: 594/10 Application for office assistant post

Dear Sir
I would like to apply for the post of office assistant
advertised in the *Weekly News*.

I am attaching my CV.

Could you please let me know that you have received this
email?

Sunita Devi

If you're sending your CV through the post, you can phone to
check it's arrived.

As I mentioned in the section about closing dates, if you send
in your application well before the closing date or time, you
will give yourself time to make sure the employer's received
it – and, if not, you'll have time to send it again.

What next?

If all goes according to plan, the employer will ask you in for
an interview. They might get in touch by:

- writing
- phoning
- emailing

regardless of how you sent your CV. The time employers take
to notify applicants about interviews can vary enormously –
from the same day to several weeks. So there is no way of
knowing how long it will be before you hear.

And, I'm afraid, it's a sad fact that if you aren't successful and
the employer isn't going to offer you an interview, you may never
hear. Some employers put a statement in their ads, such as:

> If you don't hear from us within two weeks of the closing date, please consider your application unsuccessful.

It's not very pleasant, but at least you know. Many applicants (of all ages) complain that when they apply for jobs they hear nothing. (One reason for this might be that their application never arrived, which is why it's a good idea to follow up your application, as suggested above.)

Rejection

Nobody likes to get a letter like this.

HR Department
Our Company Ltd
Somewhere
JP2 4NM

Mr J Smith
100 This Road
Somewhere
JP2 7VB

26th September 2011

Dear Mr Smith

Vacancy for Saturday Assistant
Thank you for your application. I am sorry to tell you that on this occasion your application has not been successful.

I wish you well in the future

Yours sincerely

S Jones
HR Assistant

It might feel like a kick in the teeth. But try not to take it personally. Sometimes rejection letters say something like this:

> Thank you for your application. We received a large
> number of applications for this post and I am sorry to tell
> you that on this occasion your application has not been
> successful.

or:

> Thank you for your application. We received a large
> number of applications of a very high standard for this
> post and I am sorry to tell you that on this occasion your
> application has not been successful.

Would it make you feel better or worse to know that they
'received a large number of applications of a very high standard'? It doesn't necessarily mean that yours wasn't of a high
standard. It is more likely to be something to do with the large
number of applications. The employer probably had many
suitable candidates to choose from.

The whole process of applications is likely to involve rejection
at some point. Ask anyone who has applied for vacancies –
parents, other family and friends of all ages. Most will have
had at least one rejection letter. Some people who are trying
to get into a very competitive area may have had a whole
series of rejections. So you are not alone.

You just have to keep trying. Approach each application as a
fresh attempt. Review your CV and make sure it is doing its
best for you.

- Take another look at Chapter 3 to make sure you're
  including the right information.
- Look at Chapter 5 to see if the contents are presented
  in the best way.

- Check through the points in Chapter 6 to brush up the finishing touches
- Read Chapter 8 to see what employers are looking for.
- Go through Chapter 10 to 'tailor' your CV to an individual organisation.

TIP Don't think you need to rewrite your CV completely just because you've had a rejection. Applications can sometimes seem like a matter of chance. One employer doesn't seem to be attracted by your CV, but maybe the next one will like it.

What do you know now?

- CVs can be submitted in different ways. The employer will usually tell you how they want it.
- You need to send a covering letter or email.
- Closing dates are important.

12 KEEPING TRACK

You've sent off your CV – or emailed it – to an employer and you're waiting to hear whether or not you've got an interview. Maybe you're applying to more than one employer, especially if you're looking for opportunities after you leave school – whether that's after Year 11 (S4) or Year 13 (S6).

It can be easy to lose track of your applications.

- Who have you sent CVs to?
- Who's asking for an application form?
- When are the closing dates?
- Which ones have you emailed and which ones did you send?
- Have your applications been acknowledged?

It's important to keep this sort of information in one place. If you only have one application, you will probably be able to keep the details in your head. Any more than one and it is a good idea to start keeping a written record.

This is especially true if you are tailoring your CV for each opportunity you apply for. It's worth setting up some sort of tracking system. How you do this might depend on your personality and your working style.

Some people might be happy keeping a folder for job applications on their PC. A subfolder for each employer would keep things neat – with a copy of the CV and covering letter you sent.

Alongside this (or as an alternative), if you're someone who prefers charts, it might suit you to set up something like this:

Job/ course	Source	Date of application	Date of reply	Date of interview	Notes
1					
2					
3					

Of course, again depending on your personal style, you could either do a written chart – and put it up on the wall, perhaps – or set up a table on a PC.

It all sounds very organised, but it works! Apart from anything else, this is the kind of thing you might have to do once you get to work. These days, most jobs involve some kind of administrative work – either on paper or on a computer. So it's a way of adding to your work-related skills.

TIP Tracking your applications can be good for your motivation – you will be able to see the progress of each application. If you're doing this in Year 11, 12 or 13 (S4, S5 or S6), alongside working for your GCSEs, A levels, Standard grades or Highers, this might give you more incentive to work hard and make the exams seem more relevant.

Interviews

When you send off your CV in application for a job or other opportunity, you're hoping that it'll result in an interview. If you've been asked go to for an interview, well done! It means that the CV you prepared is doing its job.

Interviews are daunting. Nearly everyone of any age gets nervous before an interview – however many interviews they may have had. You need to prepare well for an interview.

- Look again at your research about the organisation – or do a bit more.
- Check the time and venue.
- Plan your route.
- Decide what to wear.
- Re-read your CV and covering letter.
- Think about what the interviewer might ask and plan some answers.
- Think of some questions you might want to ask.

Update your CV

It's important to keep your CV completely up to date.

You will need to add any new qualifications you earn, whether from school, college or elsewhere. Remember, you don't need to wait until you've finished a qualification before including it on your CV. You can add new courses as you start them – as long as you make it clear that you haven't yet finished the course/gained the qualification. This goes for school (or college) exam courses as well as other certificates.

Here are some examples:

Qualifications				
GCSEs	English B	Science C		2009
	Maths C	Art A		
	German C	ICT B		
AS level	Applied Art (Double award)		BB	2010
BTEC	Art and Design (due for completion in 2011)			

Qualifications

Anytown High School

GCSEs	2009	English	B	Science	C
		Maths	C	Art	A
		German	C	ICT	B
DofE	2008	Bronze award			
ECDL	2008				

Anytown Sixth-Form College

AS level	2010	Applied Art (Double award)	BB
DofE	2010	Silver award	

Yourtown College (currently studying – for completion in 2011)

BTEC	BTEC Art and Design
	First Aid

Education

GCSEs	English	B	Science	C	2009
	Maths	C	Art	A	
	German	C	ICT	B	

AS level   Applied Art (Double award)   BB   2010

BTEC   Art and Design   (due for completion in 2011)

Other qualifications
Currently undertaking

Sports Leadership award (to be completed in February 2011)

It's not just qualifications which you will need to update on your CV. It's a good idea to think about your skills and experience too. You are developing skills all the time.

Grow with your CV

If you first wrote your CV in Year 11 (S4), by the time you get to Year 13 (S6) you will be quite a different person – up to two years older, with greater skills, more experience and more than likely some different attributes. As you mature, your CV needs to mature with you.

TIP When you are making changes to your CV, you may even want to have another go at some of the exercises in Chapter 4 to see whether you have a different view of yourself – or whether others see you in a new light.

Referees

It is a good idea to review your referees from time to time. Whoever you choose, and how and why you choose them, you need to be sure that the details are up to date. It's not going to help your chances of getting that job if your new employer tries to contact your referees and finds their email addresses or phone numbers have changed. The new employer won't have time to find out the new contact details. In any case, they won't see that as their job. Providing up-to-date references is up to you. If you're lucky, the new employer will get in touch with you and ask if you know where to get hold of the referee. But maybe not. Perhaps they'll just decide to offer the job to someone else.

TIP It's up to you to keep in touch with your referees and make sure their contact details are up to date.

The world rarely stands still these days – people move on in their jobs, move to new organisations or their circumstances change.

- The manager of the workshop where you did your work experience may have been promoted to a larger branch.
- Your head of year at your previous school may have retired.
- The leader at the youth club you used to go to may be on maternity leave.
- Your previous boss may have been made redundant.
- The volunteer leader may have moved house.

If the referees are people you still work with or see in school or college, then it's unlikely to be a problem. But if your referees are people from your old school, your work experience, a previous job or anywhere else you do not regularly go any more, it's worth checking the contact details from time to time. It would be polite to ask if the referees are still happy to provide references for you.

It's also worth asking yourself whether the referees on your CV are still the best people to give you a reference. Maybe you wrote your CV in Year 11 (S4) and you've now moved on elsewhere – to college or sixth-form college, perhaps. You may want to ask your present tutor or another member of staff if they would provide a reference. They have a better idea of you as you are now.

It may be useful to have more than two referees anyway. Here's an example.

Lianne wrote her CV at the beginning of Year 11 when she was looking for a weekend job. Her referees were:

- Mr Johnson, her form tutor
- Ms Bayliss, her manager on her two-week work experience in Year 10.

She asked these two people because she wanted one referee from school and one who was more work-related.

In October of Year 11, Lianne was successful in getting a weekend job. So when she needed to make applications later in Year 11, she decided to ask her boss at work if he would be a referee. He said he'd be happy to, so now Lianne has three referees. She decided she would use:

- her tutor if she applied for courses or to go to college
- her two work-related referees if she applied for jobs.

TIP Think about who you know who will provide the most useful references for you.

Storing your CV

You want to be able to use your CV, so you need to have it readily accessible (remember Greg and Lisa?). If you can store it on a PC at home then you will be able to use it and update it whenever you need to. But you may have to use a computer outside your own home – either because you do not have IT where you live (not everyone does) or because, as described above, your home system isn't exactly what you need. In this case, you may want to think about how and where you store your CV.

If you're using a system at the house of a friend or relation you may be able to access it whenever you want. But think again. What happens if your friend's out or your relation is away? You don't want this sort of thing to get in the way of any job application. You need to consider some sort of portable storage.

You may be used to storing data and documents on what I call a memory stick – but there are various names for them (flash drives, pen drives, USB drives, etc.). They have been around since about 2005, so you may not remember anything else. Compared with some of the old forms of storage such as floppy disks, they are cheap and reliable as well as easy to carry round.

TIP If you have an up-to-date CV on a memory stick, you will be able to take it wherever you need to. This means you can work on your CV on any computer – at school or college or at someone's house.

Let's say you've got a PC at home so you generally don't need to use your friend's computer. But one day, when you're at your friend's house, you start looking at job vacancies together. When you see one, you have your CV right there with you on a memory stick so you can check it's bang up to date and get it sent off straightaway, while you've got the job vacancy details in front of you.

Of course, keeping your CV on a memory stick also means you can print it out when and where you need to.

What do you know now?

- CVs need to be kept up to date.
- It's best to keep a copy of your CV on a memory stick.
- Keep in touch with your referees.

FINAL WORD

Reading this book and putting its suggestions into action will give you the tools to build yourself a really effective CV. Developing these skills now, at the beginning of your career, will set you up for job hunting and other applications throughout your working life.

Because it's not just young people who need CVs when they are starting out in their working lives. Almost everyone needs a CV at different points all through their career. I am sure you know at least one adult who is actively preparing, updating or using their CV.

There are lots of situations in which people might need to use their CV at different stages in their career. For example:

■ **A change of employer**
It's quite unusual nowadays to stay with the same employer for the whole of one's career. Many people change jobs several times in their working life – some statistics say seven times, others 11 or even more. These are averages and will vary from person to person. Reasons for changing job may include boredom, wanting more money, relocating or seeking more interesting work. Whatever the reason, each change is likely to require an up-to-date CV.

■ **A complete career change**
Some people decide to change the direction of their career completely. They may even retrain for a different trade, profession or sector. Some people do this more than once in their career. A major change like this will involve a CV.

■ **Redundancy**

This has become a sad fact of working life in recent years. The economic situation has caused some companies to collapse and others have stayed in business but only by laying off some staff. Looking for new work after redundancy means using a CV.

■ **Looking for promotion**

Even if they don't want to change employer, people may want to progress in their career and take a different, more senior, post with the same organisation. The application process in the company may be based on CVs.

■ **A return to work**

People leave the world of work for all sorts of reasons. Some they might choose – a career break to start a family or to go travelling, perhaps. Others they may not choose – family commitments, unemployment or illness, for example. At some point they will want or need to return to work and take up their career again. A CV is likely to play an important part in getting back into the workplace after a break.

■ **Becoming self-employed**

It may suit some people to work for themselves. In many sectors, people who work on a self-employed basis use their CV to seek work.

Whatever situation someone finds themselves in, they are likely to be facing competition – other people will be seeking that promotion or wanting to develop their career. In all these situations, whether they happen at the start of a career, midway through it or near the end, everyone will want to give themselves the greatest chance of success. This means having the best possible CV working as hard as it can on their behalf.

This means a CV which is:

- up to date
- complete
- well laid out
- formatted
- able to show you and your abilities to best effect
- carefully checked and proofread.

Wait a minute, that's the same list we started with in Chapter 1. Exactly! CV writing and CV skills are the same whatever age you are and whatever stage you are at in your life and work.

So the skills you are developing with the help of this book will be useful throughout your working life. Now that you are able to create a CV for yourself, you will be well-equipped to take responsibility for your working life so you are able to take control of your career.

What do you know now?

- You will need a CV throughout your career.
- How to write a CV which will attract an employer.
- How to keep your CV updated, effective and ready to use.